U.S. Department
of Transportation

**Federal Aviation
Administration**

Private Pilot – Airplane
Airman Certification Standards

June 2018

**Flight Standards Service
Washington, DC 20591**

Acknowledgments

The U.S. Department of Transportation, Federal Aviation Administration (FAA), Office of Safety Standards, Regulatory Support Division, Airman Testing Branch, P.O. Box 25082, Oklahoma City, OK 73125 developed this Airman Certification Standards (ACS) document with the assistance of the aviation community. The FAA gratefully acknowledges the valuable support from the many individuals and organizations who contributed their time and expertise to assist in this endeavor.

Availability

This ACS is available for download from www.faa.gov. Please send comments regarding this document using the following link to the Airman Testing Branch Mailbox.

Material in FAA-S-ACS-6B will be effective June 11, 2018. All previous editions of the Private Pilot – Airplane Airman Certification Standards will be obsolete as of this date for airplane applicants.

Foreword

The Federal Aviation Administration (FAA) has published the Private Pilot – Airplane Airman Certification Standards (ACS) document to communicate the aeronautical knowledge, risk management, and flight proficiency standards for the private pilot certification in the airplane category, single-engine land and sea; and multiengine land and sea classes. This ACS incorporates and supersedes FAA-S-ACS-6A, Private Pilot – Airplane Airman Certification Standards, Change 1.

The FAA views the ACS as the foundation of its transition to a more integrated and systematic approach to airman certification. The ACS is part of the safety management system (SMS) framework that the FAA uses to mitigate risks associated with airman certification training and testing. Specifically, the ACS, associated guidance, and test question components of the airman certification system are constructed around the four functional components of an SMS:

- Safety Policy that defines and describes aeronautical knowledge, flight proficiency, and risk management as integrated components of the airman certification system;
- Safety Risk Management processes through which both internal and external stakeholders identify changes in regulations, safety recommendations, or other factors. These changes are then evaluated to determine whether they require modification of airman testing and training materials;
- Safety Assurance processes to ensure the prompt and appropriate incorporation of changes arising from new regulations and safety recommendations; and
- Safety Promotion in the form of ongoing engagement with both external stakeholders (e.g., the aviation training industry) and FAA policy divisions.

The FAA has developed this ACS and its associated guidance in collaboration with a diverse group of aviation training experts. The goal is to drive a systematic approach to all components of the airman certification system, including knowledge test question development and conduct of the practical test. The FAA acknowledges and appreciates the many hours that these aviation experts have contributed toward this goal. This level of collaboration, a hallmark of a robust safety culture, strengthens and enhances aviation safety at every level of the airman certification system.

John S. Duncan
Executive Director, Flight Standards Service

Revision History

Document #	Description	Revision Date
FAA-S-8081-14B	Private Pilot Practical Test Standards for Airplane, (Changes 1-6)	November 2011
FAA-S-ACS-6	Private Pilot – Airplane Airman Certification Standards	June 1, 2016
FAA-S-ACS-6	Private Pilot – Airplane Airman Certification Standards (Change 1)	June 15, 2016
FAA-S-ACS-6A	Private Pilot – Airplane Airman Certification Standards (Change 1)	June 12, 2017
FAA-S-ACS-6B	Private Pilot – Airplane Airman Certification Standards	June 11, 2018
FAA-S-ACS-6B	Private Pilot – Airplane Airman Certification Standards (with Change 1)	June 6, 2019

Record of Changes

Change 1 (June 6, 2019)

- Revised the following sections of the <u>Introduction</u>:
  - — Airman Certification Standards Concept (page 1)
  - — Using the ACS (pages 1 and 2)

- Added FAA-H-8083-25 to list of References for Area of Operation VII, Task A. Maneuvering During Slow Flight (page 41).

- Revised Task elements corresponding to the following ACS codes to make their wording consistent with the other ACSs, as applicable:

PA.I.A.K1	PA.IV.B.S8	PA.IV.J.S6	PA.VII.D.R6
PA.I.C.K1	PA.IV.C.R4	PA.IV.K.R4	PA.VIII.A.R4
PA.I.C.K2	PA.IV.C.R6	PA.IV.K.R6	PA.VIII.B.R4
PA.I.C.K3j	PA.IV.C.S5	PA.IV.K.S5	PA.VIII.B.S2
PA.I.C.K3l	PA.IV.D.R4	PA.IV.K.S6	PA.VIII.C.R4
PA.I.C.S1	PA.IV.D.R6	PA.IV.K.S9	PA.VIII.C.S2
PA.I.C.S2	PA.IV.D.S5	PA.IV.L.R4	PA.VIII.D.R4
PA.I.C.S3	PA.IV.D.S7	PA.IV.L.R6	PA.VIII.D.S1
PA.I.E.S1	PA.IV.D.S8	PA.IV.L.S5	PA.VIII.E.R4
PA.I.E.S3	PA.IV.E.R4	PA.IV.L.S8	PA.VII.E.R7
PA.I.F.S2	PA.IV.E.R6	PA.IV.M.R2e	PA.IX.A.K1
PA.I.G.K1	PA.IV.E.S5	PA.IV.M.R3	PA.IX.A.R4
PA.I.G.S1	PA.IV.E.S11	PA.IV.M.R3a	PA.IX.A.S3
PA.I.H.K1	PA.IV.F.R4	PA.IV.M.R3b	PA.IX.B.R6
PA.I.H.K1a	PA.IV.F.R6	PA.IV.M.R4	PA.IX.C.R2
PA.I.H.K1f	PA.IV.F.S5	PA.IV.M.R6	PA.IX.E.R3
PA.I.H.R3	PA.IV.F.S7	PA.IV.N.R5	PA.IX.F.R5
PA.I.H.S1	PA.IV.F.S8	PA.IV.N.R7	PA.IX.G.K4
PA.I.I.K1	PA.IV.G.R4	PA.V.A.R2	PA.IX.G.R5
PA.II.B.S3	PA.IV.G.R6	PA.V.A.R4	PA.IX.G.S1
PA.II.D.K1	PA.IV.G.S5	PA.V.A.S2	PA.IX.G.S2
PA.II.D.S3	PA.IV.G.S9	PA.V.B.R4	PA.IX.G.S9
PA.II.E.K6b	PA.IV.G.S12	PA.VI.A.R2	PA.X.A.S7
PA.II.E.S6	PA.IV.H.R4	PA.VI.A.S4	PA.X.B.R3
PA.II.F.R4	PA.IV.H.R6	PA.VI.B.R2	PA.X.B.S6
PA.II.F.S3	PA.IV.H.S5	PA.VI.C.K2	PA.X.C.R4
PA.III.B.R2	PA.IV.H.S7	PA.VI.C.R2	PA.X.C.S11
PA.III.B.R3	PA.IV.H.S8	PA.VI.C.R4	PA.X.D.R2
PA.III.B.S1	PA.IV.I.K1	PA.VI.C.S1	PA.X.D.R3
PA.IV.A.R4	PA.IV.I.R4	PA.VI.C.S5	PA.X.D.R4
PA.IV.A.S8	PA.IV.I.R6	PA.VI.D.R2	PA.X.D.R5
PA.IV.B Objective	PA.IV.I.S7	PA.VI.D.S4	PA.X.D.R6
PA.IV.B.R1	PA.IV.I.S10	PA.VII.A.R6	PA.X.D.S1
PA.IV.B.R4	PA.IV.J.R4	PA.VII.B.R8	PA.X.D.S2
PA.IV.B.R6	PA.IV.J.R6	PA.VII.C.R8	PA.XI.A.R2
PA.IV.B.S5	PA.IV.J.S4	PA.VII.C.S4	PA.XII.A.S1

- Revised the "Knowledge Test Requirements" section of <u>Appendix 1: The Knowledge Test Eligibility, Prerequisites, and Testing Centers</u> (page A-2).

- Revised the "FAA Knowledge Test Question Coding" section of <u>Appendix 3: Airman Knowledge Test Report</u> (page A-5).

iv

- Revised the following sections of <u>Appendix 5: Practical Test Roles, Responsibilities, and Outcomes</u>:
  - Evaluator Responsibilities (page A-8)
  - Possible Outcomes of the Test (page A-9)
  - Satisfactory Performance (page A-9)
  - Testing after Discontinuance or Unsatisfactory Performance (page A-10)
  - Addition of an Airplane Single-Engine Land Rating to an existing Private Pilot Certificate (page A-12)
  - Addition of an Airplane Single-Engine Sea Rating to an existing Private Pilot Certificate (page A-13)
  - Addition of an Airplane Multiengine Land Rating to an existing Private Pilot Certificate (page A-14)
  - Addition of an Airplane Multiengine Sea Rating to an existing Private Pilot Certificate (page A-15)
- Revised the "Multiengine Considerations" section of <u>Appendix 6: Safety of Flight</u> (page A-18).
- Revised the "Equipment Requirements & Limitations" section of <u>Appendix 7: Aircraft, Equipment, and Operational Requirements & Limitations</u> (page A-19).
- Revised <u>Appendix 10: Abbreviations and Acronyms</u> (pages A-25 and A-26).

Major Enhancements to Version FAA-S-ACS-6B

- Revised Introduction and appendices to account for FAA reorganization.
- Replaced numerous prescriptive references to airplane configuration with more general references.
- Revised numerous Tasks in all Areas of Operation to include more consistent element descriptions.
- Added language to account for Part 68 BasicMed.
- Included SFRA and SATR, if applicable, in Area of Operation I, Task E.
- Distinguished different types of hypoxia in Area of Operation I, Task H.
- Broadened scope of engine starting conditions knowledge element in Area of Operation II, Task C.
- Revised Area of Operation III, Task A to include runway lighting systems.
- Revised Area of Operation IV to require touch down a proper pitch attitude.
- Restored distance tolerance in Area of Operation IV, Task B.
- Added airspeed tolerance to Area of Operation IX, Task A.
- Revised Area of Operation X, Tasks C and D to match the Instrument Rating Airman Certification Standards.
- Correlated knowledge elements of multiengine airplane engine inoperative flight to zero sideslip.
- Revised language regarding reduction of drag with one engine inoperative in terms of the manufacturer's recommendation or appropriate use of flight controls.
- Added CFIT to low altitude maneuvering risk elements.
- Added a reference to Task Objectives and enhanced *Appendix 7: Aircraft, Equipment, and Operational Requirements & Limitations*, regarding flight solely by reference to instruments.
- Updated the following Appendices:
  — Appendix 1: The Knowledge Test Eligibility, Prerequisites, and Testing Centers
  — Appendix 5: Practical Test Roles, Responsibilities, and Outcomes
  — Appendix 6: Safety of Flight
  — Appendix 7: Aircraft, Equipment, and Operational Requirements & Limitations
  — Appendix 9: References
  — Appendix 10: Abbreviations and Acronyms

Table of Contents

Introduction 1

    Airman Certification Standards Concept...1

    Using the ACS 1

I.   Preflight Preparation 3

     A.   Pilot Qualifications 3

     B.   Airworthiness Requirements..4

     C.   Weather Information 5

     D.   Cross-Country Flight Planning 6

     E.   National Airspace System...7

     F.   Performance and Limitations...8

     G.   Operation of Systems 9

     H.   Human Factors 10

     I.   Water and Seaplane Characteristics, Seaplane Bases, Maritime Rules, and Aids to Marine Navigation (ASES, AMES) 11

II.   Preflight Procedures..12

     A.   Preflight Assessment 12

     B.   Flight Deck Management 13

     C.   Engine Starting 14

     D.   Taxiing (ASEL, AMEL)..15

     E.   Taxiing and Sailing (ASES, AMES) 16

     F.   Before Takeoff Check 17

III.   Airport and Seaplane Base Operations 18

     A.   Communications, Light Signals, and Runway Lighting Systems...18

     B.   Traffic Patterns...19

IV. Takeoffs, Landings, and Go-Arounds 20

     A.   Normal Takeoff and Climb 20

     B.   Normal Approach and Landing 21

     C.   Soft-Field Takeoff and Climb (ASEL)..23

     D.   Soft-Field Approach and Landing (ASEL)..24

     E.   Short-Field Takeoff and Maximum Performance Climb (ASEL, AMEL) 25

     F.   Short-Field Approach and Landing (ASEL, AMEL)..26

     G.   Confined Area Takeoff and Maximum Performance Climb (ASES, AMES)..........................27

     H.   Confined Area Approach and Landing (ASES, AMES) 28

     I.   Glassy Water Takeoff and Climb (ASES, AMES)...29

     J.   Glassy Water Approach and Landing (ASES, AMES)...30

     K.   Rough Water Takeoff and Climb (ASES, AMES)...31

     L.   Rough Water Approach and Landing (ASES, AMES) 32

     M.   Forward Slip to a Landing (ASEL, ASES)...33

     N.   Go-Around/Rejected Landing 34

V.   Performance and Ground Reference Maneuvers...35

	A.	Steep Turns	35
	B.	Ground Reference Maneuvers	36
VI.	Navigation		37
	A.	Pilotage and Dead Reckoning	37
	B.	Navigation Systems and Radar Services	38
	C.	Diversion	39
	D.	Lost Procedures	40
VII.	Slow Flight and Stalls		41
	A.	Maneuvering During Slow Flight	41
	B.	Power-Off Stalls	42
	C.	Power-On Stalls	43
	D.	Spin Awareness	44
VIII.	Basic Instrument Maneuvers		45
	A.	Straight-and-Level Flight	45
	B.	Constant Airspeed Climbs	46
	C.	Constant Airspeed Descents	47
	D.	Turns to Headings	48
	E.	Recovery from Unusual Flight Attitudes	49
	F.	Radio Communications, Navigation Systems/Facilities, and Radar Services	50
IX.	Emergency Operations		51
	A.	Emergency Descent	51
	B.	Emergency Approach and Landing (Simulated) (ASEL, ASES)	52
	C.	Systems and Equipment Malfunctions	53
	D.	Emergency Equipment and Survival Gear	54
	E.	Engine Failure During Takeoff Before V_{MC} (Simulated) (AMEL, AMES)	55
	F.	Engine Failure After Liftoff (Simulated) (AMEL, AMES)	56
	G.	Approach and Landing with an Inoperative Engine (Simulated) (AMEL, AMES)	57
X.	Multiengine Operations		58
	A.	Maneuvering with One Engine Inoperative (AMEL, AMES)	58
	B.	V_{MC} Demonstration (AMEL, AMES)	59
	C.	One Engine Inoperative (Simulated) (solely by Reference to Instruments) During Straight-and-Level Flight and Turns (AMEL, AMES)	60
	D.	Instrument Approach and Landing with an Inoperative Engine (Simulated) (solely by Reference to Instruments) (AMEL, AMES)	61
XI.	Night Operations		62
	A.	Night Preparation	62
XII.	Postflight Procedures		63
	A.	After Landing, Parking and Securing (ASEL, AMEL)	63
	B.	Seaplane Post-Landing Procedures (ASES, AMES)	64
Appendix Table of Contents		65

Introduction

Airman Certification Standards Concept

The goal of the airman certification process is to ensure the applicant possesses the knowledge, ability to manage risks, and skill consistent with the privileges of the certificate or rating being exercised, in order to act as Pilot-in-command (PIC).

In fulfilling its responsibilities for the airman certification process, the Federal Aviation Administration (FAA) Flight Standards Service (AFS) plans, develops, and maintains materials related to airman certification training and testing. These materials include several components. The FAA knowledge test measures mastery of the aeronautical knowledge areas listed in Title 14 of the Code of Federal Regulations (14 CFR) part 61. Other materials, such as handbooks in the FAA-H-8083 series, provide guidance to applicants on aeronautical knowledge, risk management, and flight proficiency.

Safe operations in today's National Airspace System (NAS) require integration of aeronautical knowledge, risk management, and flight proficiency standards. To accomplish these goals, the FAA drew upon the expertise of organizations and individuals across the aviation and training community to develop the Airman Certification Standards (ACS). The ACS integrates the elements of knowledge, risk management, and skill listed in 14 CFR part 61 for each airman certificate or rating. It thus forms a more comprehensive standard for what an applicant must know, consider, and do for the safe conduct and successful completion of each Task to be tested on both the qualifying FAA knowledge test and the oral and flight portions of the practical test.

During the ground and flight portion of the practical test, the FAA expects evaluators to assess the applicant's mastery of the topic in accordance with the level of learning most appropriate for the specified Task. The oral questioning will continue throughout the entire practical test. For some topics, the evaluator will ask the applicant to describe or explain. For other items, the evaluator will assess the applicant's understanding by providing a scenario that requires the applicant to appropriately apply and/or correlate knowledge, experience, and information to the circumstances of the given scenario. The flight portion of the practical test requires the applicant to demonstrate knowledge, risk management, flight proficiency, and operational skill in accordance with the ACS.

Note: *As used in the ACS, an evaluator is any person authorized to conduct airman testing (e.g., an FAA Aviation Safety Inspector (ASI), Designated Pilot Examiner (DPE), or other individual authorized to conduct test for a certificate or rating).*

Using the ACS

The ACS consists of **Areas of Operation** arranged in a logical sequence, beginning with Preflight Preparation and ending with Postflight Procedures. Each Area of Operation includes **Tasks** appropriate to that Area of Operation. Each Task begins with an **Objective** stating what the applicant should know, consider, and/or do. The ACS then lists the aeronautical knowledge, risk management, and skill elements relevant to the specific Task, along with the conditions and standards for acceptable performance. The ACS uses **Notes** to emphasize special considerations. The ACS uses the terms "will" and "must" to convey directive (mandatory) information. The term "may" denotes items that are recommended but not required. The **References** for each Task indicate the source material for Task elements. For example, in Tasks such as "Weather products required for preflight planning, current and forecast weather for departure, en route, and arrival phases of flight." (PA.I.C.K2), the applicant should be prepared for questions on any weather product presented in the references for that Task.

The abbreviation(s) within parentheses immediately following a Task refer to the category and/or class airplane appropriate to that Task. The meaning of each abbreviation is as follows:

ASEL: Airplane – Single-Engine Land
ASES: Airplane – Single-Engine Sea
AMEL: Airplane – Multiengine Land
AMES: Airplane – Multiengine Sea

Note: *When administering a test, the Tasks appropriate to the class airplane (ASEL, ASES, AMEL, or AMES) used for the test must be included in the plan of action. The absence of a class indicates the Task is for all classes.*

Each Task in the ACS is coded according to a scheme that includes four elements. For example:

PA.XI.A.K1:

PA = Applicable ACS (Private Pilot – Airplane)
XI = Area of Operation (Night Operations)
A = Task (Night Preparation)
K1 = Task element Knowledge 1 (Physiological aspects of vision related to night flying.)

Knowledge test questions correspond to the ACS codes, which will ultimately replace the system of Learning Statement Codes (LSC). After this transition occurs, the Airman Knowledge Test Report (AKTR) will list an ACS code that correlates to a specific Task element for a given Area of Operation and Task. Remedial instruction and re-testing will be specific, targeted, and based on specified learning criteria. Similarly, a Notice of Disapproval for the practical test will use the ACS codes to identify the deficient Task elements. Applicants and evaluators should interpret the AKTR codes using the ACS revision in effect on the date of the knowledge test.

However, for knowledge tests taken before this system comes on line, only the LSC code (e.g., "PLT058") will be displayed on the AKTR. The LSC codes link to references and broad subject areas. By contrast, each ACS code represents a unique Task element in the ACS. Because of this fundamental difference, there is no one-to-one correlation between Learning Statement (PLT) codes and ACS codes.

Because all active knowledge test questions for the Private Pilot Airplane (PAR) Knowledge Test now align with the corresponding ACS, evaluators can use LSC codes in conjunction with this ACS for targeting retesting of missed knowledge subject areas. The evaluator should look up the LSC code(s) on the applicant's AKTR in the Learning Statement Reference Guide available using the following link: Learning Statement Reference Guide. After noting the subject area(s), the evaluator can use the corresponding Area(s) of Operation/Task(s) in the ACS to narrow the scope of material for retesting, and to evaluate the applicant's understanding of that material in the context of the appropriate ACS Area(s) of Operation and Task(s).

Applicants for a combined Private Pilot Certificate with Instrument Rating, in accordance with 14 CFR part 61, section 61.65 (a) and (g), must pass all areas designated in the Private Pilot – Airplane ACS and the Instrument Rating – Airplane ACS. Evaluators need not duplicate Tasks. For example, only one preflight demonstration would be required; however, the Preflight Task from the Instrument Rating – Airplane ACS would be more extensive than the Preflight Task from the Private Pilot – Airplane ACS to ensure readiness for Instrument Flight Rules (IFR) flight.

A combined certificate and rating evaluation should be treated as one practical test, requiring only one application and resulting in only one temporary certificate, disapproval notice, or letter of discontinuance, as applicable. Failure of any Task will result in a failure of the entire test and application. Therefore, even if the deficient maneuver was instrument related and the performance of all visual flight rules (VFR) Tasks was determined to be satisfactory, the applicant will receive a notice of disapproval.

The applicant must pass the Private Pilot Airplane (PAR) Knowledge Test before taking the private pilot practical test. The practical test is conducted in accordance with the ACS and FAA regulations that are current as of the date of the test. Further, the applicant must pass the ground portion of the practical test before beginning the flight portion.

The ground portion of the practical test allows the evaluator to determine whether the applicant is sufficiently prepared to advance to the flight portion of the practical test. The oral questioning will continue throughout the entire practical test.

Evaluators conduct the practical test in accordance with the current ACS and FAA regulations, and the FAA encourages applicants and instructors to use the ACS when preparing for knowledge tests and practical tests. The FAA will revise the ACS as circumstances require. However, if an applicant is entitled to credit for Areas of Operation previously passed as indicated on a Notice of Disapproval or Letter of Discontinuance, evaluators should continue using the ACS effective on the test cycle start date.

I. Preflight Preparation

Task	A. Pilot Qualifications
References	14 CFR parts 61, 68, 91; FAA-H-8083-2, FAA-H-8083-25; AC 68-1
Objective	To determine that the applicant exhibits satisfactory knowledge, risk management, and skills associated with airman and medical certificates including privileges, limitations, currency, and operating as pilot-in-command (PIC) as a private pilot.
Knowledge	The applicant demonstrates understanding of:
PA.I.A.K1	Certification requirements, recent flight experience, and recordkeeping.
PA.I.A.K2	Privileges and limitations.
PA.I.A.K3	Medical certificates: class, expiration, privileges, temporary disqualifications.
PA.I.A.K4	Documents required to exercise private pilot privileges.
PA.I.A.K5	Part 68 BasicMed privileges and limitations.
Risk Management	The applicant demonstrates the ability to identify, assess and mitigate risks, encompassing:
PA.I.A.R1	Failure to distinguish proficiency versus currency.
PA.I.A.R2	Flying unfamiliar airplanes, or operating with unfamiliar flight display systems, and avionics.
Skills	The applicant demonstrates the ability to:
PA.I.A.S1	Apply requirements to act as PIC under Visual Flight Rules (VFR) in a scenario given by the evaluator.

I. Preflight Preparation

Task	B. Airworthiness Requirements
References	14 CFR parts 39, 43, 91; FAA-H-8083-2, FAA-H-8083-25
Objective	To determine that the applicant exhibits satisfactory knowledge, risk management, and skills associated with airworthiness requirements, including airplane certificates.
Knowledge	The applicant demonstrates understanding of:
PA.I.B.K1	General airworthiness requirements and compliance for airplanes, including:
PA.I.B.K1a	a. Certificate location and expiration dates
PA.I.B.K1b	b. Required inspections and airplane logbook documentation
PA.I.B.K1c	c. Airworthiness Directives and Special Airworthiness Information Bulletins
PA.I.B.K1d	d. Purpose and procedure for obtaining a special flight permit
PA.I.B.K2	Pilot-performed preventive maintenance.
PA.I.B.K3	Equipment requirements for day and night VFR flight, to include:
PA.I.B.K3a	a. Flying with inoperative equipment
PA.I.B.K3b	b. Using an approved Minimum Equipment List (MEL)
PA.I.B.K3c	c. Kinds of Operation Equipment List (KOEL)
PA.I.B.K3d	d. Required discrepancy records or placards
Risk Management	The applicant demonstrates the ability to identify, assess and mitigate risks, encompassing:
PA.I.B.R1	Inoperative equipment discovered prior to flight.
Skills	The applicant demonstrates the ability to:
PA.I.B.S1	Locate and describe airplane airworthiness and registration information.
PA.I.B.S2	Determine the airplane is airworthy in a scenario given by the evaluator.
PA.I.B.S3	Apply appropriate procedures for operating with inoperative equipment in a scenario given by the evaluator.

I. Preflight Preparation

Task	C. *Weather Information*
References	14 CFR part 91; FAA-H-8083-25; AC 00-6, AC 00-45, <u>AC 00-54;</u> AIM
Objective	To determine that the applicant exhibits satisfactory knowledge, risk management, and skills associated with weather information for a flight under VFR.
Knowledge	The applicant demonstrates understanding of:
PA.I.C.K1	Sources of weather data (e.g., National Weather Service, Flight Service) for flight planning purposes.
PA.I.C.K2	Acceptable weather products and resources required for preflight planning, current and forecast weather for departure, en route, and arrival phases of flight.
PA.I.C.K3	Meteorology applicable to the departure, en route, alternate, and destination under VFR in Visual Meteorological Conditions (VMC) to include expected climate and hazardous conditions such as:
PA.I.C.K3a	a. Atmospheric composition and stability
PA.I.C.K3b	b. Wind (e.g., crosswind, tailwind, windshear, <u>mountain wave,</u> etc.)
PA.I.C.K3c	c. Temperature
PA.I.C.K3d	d. Moisture/precipitation
PA.I.C.K3e	e. Weather system formation, including air masses and fronts
PA.I.C.K3f	f. Clouds
PA.I.C.K3g	g. Turbulence
PA.I.C.K3h	h. Thunderstorms and microbursts
PA.I.C.K3i	i. Icing and freezing level information
PA.I.C.K3j	j. Fog/mist
PA.I.C.K3k	k. Frost
PA.I.C.K3l	l. Obstructions to visibility (e.g., smoke, haze, volcanic ash, etc.)
PA.I.C.K4	Flight deck displays of digital weather and aeronautical information.
Risk Management	The applicant demonstrates the ability to identify, assess and mitigate risks, encompassing:
PA.I.C.R1	Factors involved in making the go/no-go and continue/divert decisions, to include:
PA.I.C.R1a	a. Circumstances that would make diversion prudent
PA.I.C.R1b	b. Personal weather minimums
PA.I.C.R1c	c. Hazardous weather conditions to include known or forecast icing or turbulence aloft
PA.I.C.R2	Limitations of:
PA.I.C.R2a	a. Onboard weather equipment
PA.I.C.R2b	b. Aviation weather reports and forecasts
PA.I.C.R2c	c. Inflight weather resources
Skills	The applicant demonstrates the ability to:
PA.I.C.S1	Use available aviation weather resources to obtain an adequate weather briefing.
PA.I.C.S2	Analyze the implications of at least three of the conditions listed in K3a through K3l above, using actual weather or weather conditions in a scenario provided by the evaluator.
PA.I.C.S3	Correlate weather information to make a competent go/no-go decision.

I. Preflight Preparation

Task	D. Cross-Country Flight Planning
References	14 CFR part 91; FAA-H-8083-2, FAA-H-8083-25; Navigation Charts; Chart Supplements; AIM; NOTAMs
Objective	To determine that the applicant exhibits satisfactory knowledge, risk management, and skills associated with cross-country flights and VFR flight planning.
Knowledge	The applicant demonstrates understanding of:
PA.I.D.K1	Route planning, including consideration of different classes and special use airspace (SUA) and selection of appropriate and available navigation/communication systems and facilities.
PA.I.D.K2	Altitude selection accounting for terrain and obstacles, glide distance of the airplane, VFR cruising altitudes, and the effect of wind.
PA.I.D.K3	Calculating:
PA.I.D.K3a	a. Time, climb and descent rates, course, distance, heading, true airspeed, and groundspeed
PA.I.D.K3b	b. Estimated time of arrival to include conversion to universal coordinated time (UTC)
PA.I.D.K3c	c. Fuel requirements, to include reserve
PA.I.D.K4	Elements of a VFR flight plan.
PA.I.D.K5	Procedures for activating and closing a VFR flight plan.
Risk Management	The applicant demonstrates the ability to identify, assess and mitigate risks, encompassing:
PA.I.D.R1	Pilot.
PA.I.D.R2	Aircraft.
PA.I.D.R3	Environment (e.g., weather, airports, airspace, terrain, obstacles).
PA.I.D.R4	External pressures.
PA.I.D.R5	Limitations of air traffic control (ATC) services.
PA.I.D.R6	Improper fuel planning.
Skills	The applicant demonstrates the ability to:
PA.I.D.S1	Prepare, present, and explain a cross-country flight plan assigned by the evaluator including a risk analysis based on real-time weather, to the first fuel stop.
PA.I.D.S2	Apply pertinent information from appropriate and current aeronautical charts, Chart Supplements; NOTAMs relative to airport, runway and taxiway closures; and other flight publications.
PA.I.D.S3	Create a navigation plan and simulate filing a VFR flight plan.
PA.I.D.S4	Recalculate fuel reserves based on a scenario provided by the evaluator.

I.   Preflight Preparation

Task	E. National Airspace System
References	14 CFR parts 71, 91, 93; FAA-H-8083-2; Navigation Charts; AIM
Objective	To determine that the applicant exhibits satisfactory knowledge, risk management, and skills associated with the National Airspace System (NAS) operating under VFR as a private pilot.
Knowledge	The applicant demonstrates understanding of:
PA.I.E.K1	Types of airspace/airspace classes and associated requirements and limitations.
PA.I.E.K2	Charting symbology.
PA.I.E.K3	Special use airspace (SUA), special flight rules areas (SFRA), temporary flight restrictions (TFR), and other airspace areas.
Risk Management	The applicant demonstrates the ability to identify, assess and mitigate risks, encompassing:
PA.I.E.R1	Various classes and types of airspace.
Skills	The applicant demonstrates the ability to:
PA.I.E.S1	Identify and comply with the requirements for basic VFR weather minimums and flying in particular classes of airspace.
PA.I.E.S2	Correctly identify airspace and operate in accordance with associated communication and equipment requirements.
PA.I.E.S3	Identify the requirements for operating in SUA or within a TFR. Identify and comply with SATR and SFRA operations, if applicable.

I. Preflight Preparation

Task	F. *Performance and Limitations*
References	FAA-H-8083-1, FAA-H-8083-2, FAA-H-8083-3, FAA-H-8083-25; POH/AFM
Objective	To determine that the applicant exhibits satisfactory knowledge, risk management, and skills associated with operating an airplane safely within the parameters of its performance capabilities and limitations.
Knowledge	The applicant demonstrates understanding of:
PA.I.F.K1	Elements related to performance and limitations by explaining the use of charts, tables, and data to determine performance.
PA.I.F.K2	Factors affecting performance, to include:
PA.I.F.K2a	a. Atmospheric conditions
PA.I.F.K2b	b. Pilot technique
PA.I.F.K2c	c. Airplane configuration
PA.I.F.K2d	d. Airport environment
PA.I.F.K2e	e. Loading (e.g., center of gravity)
PA.I.F.K2f	f. Weight and balance
PA.I.F.K3	Aerodynamics.
Risk Management	The applicant demonstrates the ability to identify, assess and mitigate risks, encompassing:
PA.I.F.R1	Inaccurate use of manufacturer's performance charts, tables, and data.
PA.I.F.R2	Exceeding airplane limitations.
PA.I.F.R3	Possible differences between calculated performance and actual performance.
Skills	The applicant demonstrates the ability to:
PA.I.F.S1	Compute the weight and balance, correct out-of-center of gravity (CG) loading errors and determine if the weight and balance remains within limits during all phases of flight.
PA.I.F.S2	Utilize the appropriate airplane manufacturer's approved performance charts, tables, and data.

I.   Preflight Preparation

Task	G. Operation of Systems
References	FAA-H-8083-2, FAA-H-8083-3, FAA-H-8083-23, FAA-H-8083-25; POH/AFM.
Objective	To determine that the applicant exhibits satisfactory knowledge, risk management, and skills associated with the safe operation of systems on the airplane provided for the flight test.
Knowledge	The applicant demonstrates understanding of:
PA.I.G.K1	Airplane systems, to include: **Note:** If K1 is selected, the evaluator must assess the applicant's knowledge of at least three of the following sub-elements.
PA.I.G.K1a	a. Primary flight controls
PA.I.G.K1b	b. Secondary flight controls
PA.I.G.K1c	c. Powerplant and propeller
PA.I.G.K1d	d. Landing gear
PA.I.G.K1e	e. Fuel, oil, and hydraulic
PA.I.G.K1f	f. Electrical
PA.I.G.K1g	g. Avionics
PA.I.G.K1h	h. Pitot-static, vacuum/pressure, and associated flight instruments
PA.I.G.K1i	i. Environmental
PA.I.G.K1j	j. Deicing and anti-icing
PA.I.G.K1k	k. Water rudders (ASES, AMES)
PA.I.G.K1l	l. Oxygen system
PA.I.G.K2	Indications of and procedures for managing system abnormalities or failures.
Risk Management	The applicant demonstrates the ability to identify, assess and mitigate risks, encompassing:
PA.I.G.R1	Failure to detect system malfunctions or failures.
PA.I.G.R2	Improper management of a system failure.
PA.I.G.R3	Failure to monitor and manage automated systems.
Skills	The applicant demonstrates the ability to:
PA.I.G.S1	Operate at least three of the systems listed in K1a through K1l above appropriately.
PA.I.G.S2	Use appropriate checklists properly.

I. Preflight Preparation

Task	H. Human Factors
References	FAA-H-8083-2, FAA-H-8083-25; AIM
Objective	To determine that the applicant exhibits satisfactory knowledge, risk management, and skills associated with personal health, flight physiology, aeromedical and human factors, as it relates to safety of flight. **Note:** See _Appendix 6: Safety of Flight_.
Knowledge	The applicant demonstrates understanding of:
PA.I.H.K1	The symptoms (as applicable), recognition, causes, effects, and corrective actions associated with aeromedical and physiological issues including:
PA.I.H.K1a	a. Hypoxia
PA.I.H.K1b	b. Hyperventilation
PA.I.H.K1c	c. Middle ear and sinus problems
PA.I.H.K1d	d. Spatial disorientation
PA.I.H.K1e	e. Motion sickness
PA.I.H.K1f	f. Carbon monoxide poisoning
PA.I.H.K1g	g. Stress
PA.I.H.K1h	h. Fatigue
PA.I.H.K1i	i. Dehydration and nutrition
PA.I.H.K1j	j. Hypothermia
PA.I.H.K1k	k. Optical illusions
PA.I.H.K1l	l. Dissolved nitrogen in the bloodstream after scuba dives
PA.I.H.K2	Regulations regarding use of alcohol and drugs.
PA.I.H.K3	Effects of alcohol, drugs, and over-the-counter medications.
PA.I.H.K4	Aeronautical Decision-Making (ADM).
Risk Management	The applicant demonstrates the ability to identify, assess and mitigate risks encompassing:
PA.I.H.R1	Aeromedical and physiological issues.
PA.I.H.R2	Hazardous attitudes.
PA.I.H.R3	Distractions, loss of situational awareness, or improper task management.
Skills	The applicant demonstrates the ability to:
PA.I.H.S1	Associate the symptoms and effects for at least three of the conditions listed in K1a through K1l above with the cause(s) and corrective action(s).
PA.I.H.S2	Perform self-assessment, including fitness for flight and personal minimums, for actual flight or a scenario given by the evaluator.

I.   Preflight Preparation

Task	I. *Water and Seaplane Characteristics, Seaplane Bases, Maritime Rules, and Aids to Marine Navigation (ASES, AMES)*
References	FAA-H-8083-2, FAA-H-8083-23; AIM; USCG Navigation Rules, International-Inland; POH/AFM; Chart Supplements
Objective	To determine that the applicant exhibits satisfactory knowledge, risk management, and skills associated with water and seaplane characteristics, seaplane bases, maritime rules, and aids to marine navigation.
Knowledge	The applicant demonstrates understanding of:
PA.I.I.K1	The characteristics of a water surface as affected by features, such as:
PA.I.I.K1a	a. Size and location
PA.I.I.K1b	b. Protected and unprotected areas
PA.I.I.K1c	c. Surface wind
PA.I.I.K1d	d. Direction and strength of water current
PA.I.I.K1e	e. Floating and partially submerged debris
PA.I.I.K1f	f. Sandbars, islands, and shoals
PA.I.I.K1g	g. Vessel traffic and wakes
PA.I.I.K1h	h. Other characteristics specific to the area
PA.I.I.K2	Float and hull construction, and its effect on seaplane performance.
PA.I.I.K3	Causes of porpoising and skipping, and the pilot action needed to prevent or correct these occurrences.
PA.I.I.K4	How to locate and identify seaplane bases on charts or in directories.
PA.I.I.K5	Operating restrictions at various bases.
PA.I.I.K6	Right-of-way, steering, and sailing rules pertinent to seaplane operation.
PA.I.I.K7	Marine navigation aids, such as buoys, beacons, lights, sound signals, and range markers.
Risk Management	The applicant demonstrates the ability to identify, assess and mitigate risks, encompassing:
PA.I.I.R1	Local conditions.
PA.I.I.R2	Impact of marine traffic.
Skills	The applicant demonstrates the ability to:
PA.I.I.S1	Assess the water surface characteristics for the proposed flight.
PA.I.I.S2	Identify restrictions at local seaplane bases.
PA.I.I.S3	Identify marine navigation aids.
PA.I.I.S4	Perform correct right-of-way, steering, and sailing operations.

II. Preflight Procedures

Task	A. *Preflight Assessment*
References	FAA-H-8083-2, FAA-H-8083-3, FAA-H-8083-23; POH/AFM; AC 00-6
Objective	To determine that the applicant exhibits satisfactory knowledge, risk management, and skills associated with preparing for safe flight.
Knowledge	The applicant demonstrates understanding of:
PA.II.A.K1	Pilot self-assessment.
PA.II.A.K2	Determining that the airplane to be used is appropriate and airworthy.
PA.II.A.K3	Airplane preflight inspection including:
PA.II.A.K3a	a. Which items must be inspected
PA.II.A.K3b	b. The reasons for checking each item
PA.II.A.K3c	c. How to detect possible defects
PA.II.A.K3d	d. The associated regulations
PA.II.A.K4	Environmental factors including weather, terrain, route selection, and obstructions.
Risk Management	The applicant demonstrates the ability to identify, assess and mitigate risks, encompassing:
PA.II.A.R1	Pilot.
PA.II.A.R2	Aircraft.
PA.II.A.R3	Environment (e.g., weather, airports, airspace, terrain, obstacles).
PA.II.A.R4	External pressures.
PA.II.A.R5	Aviation security concerns.
Skills	The applicant demonstrates the ability to:
PA.II.A.S1	Inspect the airplane with reference to an appropriate checklist.
PA.II.A.S2	Verify the airplane is in condition for safe flight and conforms to its type design.

II. Preflight Procedures

Task	B. Flight Deck Management
References	FAA-H-8083-2, FAA-H-8083-3; AC 120-71; POH/AFM
Objective	To determine that the applicant exhibits satisfactory knowledge, risk management, and skills associated with safe flight deck management practices.
Knowledge	The applicant demonstrates understanding of:
PA.II.B.K1	Passenger briefing requirements, to include operation and required use of safety restraint systems.
PA.II.B.K2	Use of appropriate checklists.
PA.II.B.K3	Requirements for current and appropriate navigation data.
Risk Management	The applicant demonstrates the ability to identify, assess and mitigate risks, encompassing:
PA.II.B.R1	Improper use of systems or equipment, to include automation and portable electronic devices.
PA.II.B.R2	Flying with unresolved discrepancies.
Skills	The applicant demonstrates the ability to:
PA.II.B.S1	Secure all items in the flight deck and cabin.
PA.II.B.S2	Conduct an appropriate pre-takeoff briefing, to include identifying the PIC, use of safety belts, shoulder harnesses, doors, sterile flight deck, and emergency procedures.
PA.II.B.S3	Program and manage the airplane's automation properly.

II. Preflight Procedures

Task	C. Engine Starting
References	FAA-H-8083-2, FAA-H-8083-3, FAA-H-8083-25; POH/AFM
Objective	To determine that the applicant exhibits satisfactory knowledge, risk management, and skills associated with recommended engine starting procedures.
Knowledge	The applicant demonstrates understanding of:
PA.II.C.K1	Starting under various conditions.
PA.II.C.K2	Starting the engine(s) by use of external power.
PA.II.C.K3	Engine limitations as they relate to starting.
Risk Management	The applicant demonstrates the ability to identify, assess and mitigate risks, encompassing:
PA.II.C.R1	Propeller safety.
Skills	The applicant demonstrates the ability to:
PA.II.C.S1	Position the airplane properly considering structures, other aircraft, wind, and the safety of nearby persons and property.
PA.II.C.S2	Complete the appropriate checklist.

II. Preflight Procedures

Task	D. Taxiing (ASEL, AMEL)
References	FAA-H-8083-2, FAA-H-8083-3, FAA-H-8083-25; POH/AFM; AC 91-73; Chart Supplements; AIM
Objective	To determine that the applicant exhibits satisfactory knowledge, risk management, and skills associated with safe taxi operations, including runway incursion avoidance.
Knowledge	The applicant demonstrates understanding of:
PA.II.D.K1	Current airport aeronautical references and information resources such as the Chart Supplement, airport diagram, and NOTAMS.
PA.II.D.K2	Taxi instructions/clearances.
PA.II.D.K3	Airport markings, signs, and lights.
PA.II.D.K4	Visual indicators for wind.
PA.II.D.K5	Aircraft lighting.
PA.II.D.K6	Procedures for:
PA.II.D.K6a	a. Appropriate flight deck activities prior to taxi, including route planning and identifying the location of Hot Spots
PA.II.D.K6b	b. Radio communications at towered and nontowered airports
PA.II.D.K6c	c. Entering or crossing runways
PA.II.D.K6d	d. Night taxi operations
PA.II.D.K6e	e. Low visibility taxi operations
Risk Management	The applicant demonstrates the ability to identify, assess and mitigate risks, encompassing:
PA.II.D.R1	Inappropriate activities and distractions.
PA.II.D.R2	Confirmation or expectation bias as related to taxi instructions.
PA.II.D.R3	A taxi route or departure runway change.
Skills	The applicant demonstrates the ability to:
PA.II.D.S1	Receive and correctly read back clearances/instructions, if applicable.
PA.II.D.S2	Use an airport diagram or taxi chart during taxi, if published, and maintain situational awareness.
PA.II.D.S3	Position the flight controls for the existing wind.
PA.II.D.S4	Complete the appropriate checklist.
PA.II.D.S5	Perform a brake check immediately after the airplane begins moving.
PA.II.D.S6	Maintain positive control of the airplane during ground operations by controlling direction and speed without excessive use of brakes.
PA.II.D.S7	Comply with airport/taxiway markings, signals, and ATC clearances and instructions.
PA.II.D.S8	Position the airplane properly relative to hold lines.

II. Preflight Procedures

Task	E. Taxiing and Sailing (ASES, AMES)
References	FAA-H-8083-2, FAA-H-8083-23, FAA-H-8083-25; POH/AFM; AC 91-73; Chart Supplements; AIM
Objective	To determine that the applicant exhibits satisfactory knowledge, risk management, and skills associated with safe taxiing and sailing operations, including runway incursion avoidance.
Knowledge	The applicant demonstrates understanding of:
PA.II.E.K1	Airport information resources including Chart Supplements, airport diagram, and appropriate references.
PA.II.E.K2	Taxi instructions/clearances.
PA.II.E.K3	Airport/seaplane base markings, signs, and lights.
PA.II.E.K4	Visual indicators for wind.
PA.II.E.K5	Airplane lighting.
PA.II.E.K6	Procedures for:
PA.II.E.K6a	a. Appropriate flight deck activities during taxiing or sailing
PA.II.E.K6b	b. Radio communications at towered and nontowered seaplane bases
Risk Management	The applicant demonstrates the ability to identify, assess and mitigate risks, encompassing:
PA.II.E.R1	Inappropriate activities and distractions.
PA.II.E.R2	Porpoising and skipping.
PA.II.E.R3	Low visibility taxi and sailing operations.
PA.II.E.R4	Other aircraft, vessels, and hazards.
Skills	The applicant demonstrates the ability to:
PA.II.E.S1	Receive and correctly read back clearances/instructions, if applicable.
PA.II.E.S2	Use an appropriate diagram or chart during taxi, if published.
PA.II.E.S3	Comply with seaplane base/airport/taxiway markings, signals, and signs.
PA.II.E.S4	Depart the dock/mooring buoy or beach/ramp in a safe manner, considering wind, current, traffic, and hazards.
PA.II.E.S5	Complete the appropriate checklist.
PA.II.E.S6	Position the flight controls, flaps, doors, water rudders, and power correctly for the existing conditions to follow the desired course while sailing and to prevent or correct for porpoising and skipping during step taxi.
PA.II.E.S7	Exhibit procedures for steering and maneuvering while maintaining proper situational awareness and desired orientation, path, and position while taxiing using idle, plow, or step taxi technique, as appropriate.
PA.II.E.S8	Plan and follow the most favorable taxi or sailing course for current conditions.
PA.II.E.S9	Abide by right-of-way rules, maintain positive airplane control, proper speed, and separation between other aircraft, vessels, and persons.
PA.II.E.S10	Comply with applicable taxi elements in Task D if the practical test *is conducted* in an amphibious airplane.

II.   Preflight Procedures

Task	F. Before Takeoff Check
References	FAA-H-8083-2, FAA-H-8083-3, FAA-H-8083-23; POH/AFM
Objective	To determine that the applicant exhibits satisfactory knowledge, risk management, and skills associated with the before takeoff check.
Knowledge	The applicant demonstrates understanding of:
PA.II.F.K1	Purpose of pre-takeoff checklist items including:
PA.II.F.K1a	a. Reasons for checking each item
PA.II.F.K1b	b. Detecting malfunctions
PA.II.F.K1c	c. Ensuring the airplane is in safe operating condition as recommended by the manufacturer
Risk Management	The applicant demonstrates the ability to identify, assess and mitigate risks, encompassing:
PA.II.F.R1	Division of attention while conducting pre-flight checks.
PA.II.F.R2	Unexpected runway changes by ATC.
PA.II.F.R3	Wake turbulence.
PA.II.F.R4	A powerplant failure during takeoff or other malfunction considering operational factors such as airplane characteristics, runway/takeoff path length, surface conditions, environmental conditions, and obstructions.
Skills	The applicant demonstrates the ability to:
PA.II.F.S1	Review takeoff performance.
PA.II.F.S2	Complete the appropriate checklist.
PA.II.F.S3	Position the airplane appropriately considering other aircraft, vessels, and wind.
PA.II.F.S4	Divide attention inside and outside the flight deck.
PA.II.F.S5	Verify that engine parameters and airplane configuration are suitable.

III. Airport and Seaplane Base Operations

Task	A. Communications, Light Signals, and Runway Lighting Systems
References	14 CFR part 91; FAA-H-8083-2, FAA-H-8083-25; AIM
Objective	To determine that the applicant exhibits satisfactory knowledge, risk management, and skills associated with normal and emergency radio communications, ATC light signals, and runway lighting systems to conduct safe airport operations.
Knowledge	The applicant demonstrates understanding of:
PA.III.A.K1	How to obtain proper radio frequencies.
PA.III.A.K2	Proper radio communication procedures and ATC phraseology.
PA.III.A.K3	ATC light signal recognition.
PA.III.A.K4	Appropriate use of transponders.
PA.III.A.K5	Lost communication procedures.
PA.III.A.K6	Equipment issues that could cause loss of communication.
PA.III.A.K7	Radar assistance.
PA.III.A.K8	National Transportation Safety Board (NTSB) accident/incident reporting.
PA.III.A.K9	Runway Status Lighting Systems.
Risk Management	The applicant demonstrates the ability to identify, assess and mitigate risks, encompassing:
PA.III.A.R1	Poor communication.
PA.III.A.R2	Failure to recognize and declare an emergency.
PA.III.A.R3	Confirmation or expectation bias.
Skills	The applicant demonstrates the ability to:
PA.III.A.S1	Select appropriate frequencies.
PA.III.A.S2	Transmit using phraseology and procedures as specified in the AIM.
PA.III.A.S3	Acknowledge radio communications and comply with instructions.

III. Airport and Seaplane Base Operations

Task	B. *Traffic Patterns*
References	14 CFR part 91; FAA-H-8083-2, FAA-H-8083-25; AIM
Objective	To determine that the applicant exhibits satisfactory knowledge, risk management, and skills associated with traffic patterns.
Knowledge	The applicant demonstrates understanding of:
PA.III.B.K1	Towered and nontowered airport operations.
PA.III.B.K2	Runway selection for the current conditions.
PA.III.B.K3	Right-of-way rules.
PA.III.B.K4	Use of automated weather and airport information.
Risk Management	The applicant demonstrates the ability to identify, assess and mitigate risks, encompassing:
PA.III.B.R1	Collision hazards, to include aircraft, terrain, obstacles, and wires.
PA.III.B.R2	Distractions, loss of situational awareness, or improper task management.
PA.III.B.R3	Wake turbulence or windshear.
Skills	The applicant demonstrates the ability to:
PA.III.B.S1	Identify and interpret airport/seaplane base runways, taxiways, markings, signs, and lighting.
PA.III.B.S2	Comply with recommended traffic pattern procedures.
PA.III.B.S3	Correct for wind drift to maintain the proper ground track.
PA.III.B.S4	Maintain orientation with the runway/landing area in use.
PA.III.B.S5	Maintain traffic pattern altitude, ±100 feet, and the appropriate airspeed, ±10 knots.
PA.III.B.S6	Maintain situational awareness and proper spacing from other aircraft in the traffic pattern.

IV. Takeoffs, Landings, and Go-Arounds

Task	A. Normal Takeoff and Climb
References	FAA-H-8083-2, FAA-H-8083-3, FAA-H-8083-23; POH/AFM; AIM
Objective	To determine that the applicant exhibits satisfactory knowledge, risk management, and skills associated with a normal takeoff, climb operations, and rejected takeoff procedures. **Note:** *If a crosswind condition does not exist, the applicant's knowledge of crosswind elements must be evaluated through oral testing.*
Knowledge	The applicant demonstrates understanding of:
PA.IV.A.K1	Effects of atmospheric conditions, including wind, on takeoff and climb performance.
PA.IV.A.K2	V_X and V_Y.
PA.IV.A.K3	Appropriate airplane configuration.
Risk Management	The applicant demonstrates the ability to identify, assess and mitigate risks, encompassing:
PA.IV.A.R1	Selection of runway based on pilot capability, airplane performance and limitations, available distance, and wind.
PA.IV.A.R2	Effects of:
PA.IV.A.R2a	a. Crosswind
PA.IV.A.R2b	b. Windshear
PA.IV.A.R2c	c. Tailwind
PA.IV.A.R2d	d. Wake turbulence
PA.IV.A.R2e	e. Runway surface/condition
PA.IV.A.R3	Abnormal operations, to include planning for:
PA.IV.A.R3a	a. Rejected takeoff
PA.IV.A.R3b	b. Engine failure in takeoff/climb phase of flight
PA.IV.A.R4	Collision hazards, to include aircraft, terrain, obstacles, wires, vehicles, vessels, persons, and wildlife.
PA.IV.A.R5	Low altitude maneuvering including stall, spin, or CFIT.
PA.IV.A.R6	Distractions, loss of situational awareness, or improper task management.
Skills	The applicant demonstrates the ability to:
PA.IV.A.S1	Complete the appropriate checklist.
PA.IV.A.S2	Make radio calls as appropriate.
PA.IV.A.S3	Verify assigned/correct runway.
PA.IV.A.S4	Ascertain wind direction with or without visible wind direction indicators.
PA.IV.A.S5	Position the flight controls for the existing wind.
PA.IV.A.S6	Clear the area; taxi into takeoff position and align the airplane on the runway centerline (ASEL, AMEL) or takeoff path (ASES, AMES).
PA.IV.A.S7	Confirm takeoff power and proper engine and flight instrument indications prior to rotation (ASEL, AMEL).
PA.IV.A.S8	Avoid excessive water spray on the propeller(s) (ASES, AMES).
PA.IV.A.S9	Rotate and lift off at the recommended airspeed and accelerate to V_Y.
PA.IV.A.S10	Retract the water rudders, as appropriate, establish and maintain the most efficient planing/liftoff attitude, and correct for porpoising and skipping (ASES, AMES).
PA.IV.A.S11	Establish a pitch attitude to maintain the manufacturer's recommended speed or V_Y, +10/-5 knots.
PA.IV.A.S12	Configure the airplane in accordance with manufacturer's guidance.
PA.IV.A.S13	Maintain V_Y +10/-5 knots to a safe maneuvering altitude.
PA.IV.A.S14	Maintain directional control and proper wind-drift correction throughout takeoff and climb.
PA.IV.A.S15	Comply with noise abatement procedures.

IV. Takeoffs, Landings, and Go-Arounds

Task	B. Normal Approach and Landing
References	FAA-H-8083-2, FAA-H-8083-3, FAA-H-8083-23; POH/AFM; AIM
Objective	To determine that the applicant exhibits satisfactory knowledge, risk management, and skills associated with a normal approach and landing with emphasis on proper use of flight controls. *Note:* If a crosswind condition does not exist, the applicant's knowledge of crosswind elements must be evaluated through oral testing.
Knowledge	The applicant demonstrates understanding of:
PA.IV.B.K1	A stabilized approach, to include energy management concepts.
PA.IV.B.K2	Effects of atmospheric conditions, including wind, on approach and landing performance.
PA.IV.B.K3	Wind correction techniques on approach and landing.
Risk Management	The applicant demonstrates the ability to identify, assess and mitigate risks, encompassing:
PA.IV.B.R1	Selection of runway or approach path and touchdown area based on pilot capability, airplane performance and limitations, available distance, and wind.
PA.IV.B.R2	Effects of:
PA.IV.B.R2a	a. Crosswind
PA.IV.B.R2b	b. Windshear
PA.IV.B.R2c	c. Tailwind
PA.IV.B.R2d	d. Wake turbulence
PA.IV.B.R2e	e. Runway surface/condition
PA.IV.B.R3	Planning for:
PA.IV.B.R3a	a. Go-around and rejected landing
PA.IV.B.R3b	b. Land and hold short operations (LAHSO)
PA.IV.B.R4	Collision hazards, to include aircraft, terrain, obstacles, wires, vehicles, vessels, persons, and wildlife.
PA.IV.B.R5	Low altitude maneuvering including stall, spin, or CFIT.
PA.IV.B.R6	Distractions, loss of situational awareness, incorrect airport surface approach and landing, or improper task management.
Skills	The applicant demonstrates the ability to:
PA.IV.B.S1	Complete the appropriate checklist.
PA.IV.B.S2	Make radio calls as appropriate.
PA.IV.B.S3	Ensure the airplane is aligned with the correct/assigned runway or landing surface.
PA.IV.B.S4	Scan runway or landing surface and the adjoining area for traffic and obstructions.
PA.IV.B.S5	Select and aim for a suitable touchdown point considering the wind, landing surface, and obstructions.
PA.IV.B.S6	Establish the recommended approach and landing configuration and airspeed, and adjust pitch attitude and power as required to maintain a stabilized approach.
PA.IV.B.S7	Maintain manufacturer's published approach airspeed or in its absence not more than 1.3 V_{SO}, +10/-5 knots with gust factor applied.
PA.IV.B.S8	Maintain directional control and appropriate crosswind correction throughout the approach and landing.
PA.IV.B.S9	Make smooth, timely, and correct control application during round out and touchdown.
PA.IV.B.S10	Touch down at a proper pitch attitude, within 400 feet beyond or on the specified point, with no side drift, and with the airplane's longitudinal axis aligned with and over the runway center/landing path.
PA.IV.B.S11	Execute a timely go-around if the approach cannot be made within the tolerances specified above or for any other condition that may result in an unsafe approach or landing.
PA.IV.B.S12	Utilize runway incursion avoidance procedures.

IV. Takeoffs, Landings, and Go-Arounds

IV. Takeoffs, Landings, and Go-Arounds

Task	C. Soft-Field Takeoff and Climb (ASEL)
References	FAA-H-8083-2, FAA-H-8083-3; POH/AFM; AIM
Objective	To determine that the applicant exhibits satisfactory knowledge, risk management, and skills associated with a soft-field takeoff, climb operations, and rejected takeoff procedures.
Knowledge	The applicant demonstrates understanding of:
PA.IV.C.K1	Effects of atmospheric conditions, including wind, on takeoff and climb performance.
PA.IV.C.K2	V_X and V_Y.
PA.IV.C.K3	Appropriate airplane configuration.
PA.IV.C.K4	Ground effect.
PA.IV.C.K5	Importance of weight transfer from wheels to wings.
PA.IV.C.K6	Left turning tendencies.
Risk Management	The applicant demonstrates the ability to identify, assess and mitigate risks, encompassing:
PA.IV.C.R1	Selection of runway based on pilot capability, airplane performance and limitations, available distance, and wind.
PA.IV.C.R2	Effects of:
PA.IV.C.R2a	a. Crosswind
PA.IV.C.R2b	b. Windshear
PA.IV.C.R2c	c. Tailwind
PA.IV.C.R2d	d. Wake turbulence
PA.IV.C.R2e	e. Runway surface/condition
PA.IV.C.R3	Abnormal operations, to include planning for:
PA.IV.C.R3a	a. Rejected takeoff
PA.IV.C.R3b	b. Engine failure in takeoff/climb phase of flight
PA.IV.C.R4	Collision hazards, to include aircraft, terrain, obstacles, wires, vehicles, persons, and wildlife.
PA.IV.C.R5	Low altitude maneuvering including stall, spin, or CFIT.
PA.IV.C.R6	Distractions, loss of situational awareness, or improper task management.
Skills	The applicant demonstrates the ability to:
PA.IV.C.S1	Complete the appropriate checklist.
PA.IV.C.S2	Make radio calls as appropriate.
PA.IV.C.S3	Verify assigned/correct runway.
PA.IV.C.S4	Ascertain wind direction with or without visible wind direction indicators.
PA.IV.C.S5	Position the flight controls for the existing wind.
PA.IV.C.S6	Clear the area, maintain necessary flight control inputs, taxi into takeoff position and align the airplane on the runway centerline without stopping, while advancing the throttle smoothly to takeoff power.
PA.IV.C.S7	Confirm takeoff power and proper engine and flight instrument indications.
PA.IV.C.S8	Establish and maintain a pitch attitude that will transfer the weight of the airplane from the wheels to the wings as rapidly as possible.
PA.IV.C.S9	Lift off at the lowest possible airspeed and remain in ground effect while accelerating to V_X or V_Y, as appropriate.
PA.IV.C.S10	Establish a pitch attitude for V_X or V_Y, as appropriate, and maintain selected airspeed +10/-5 knots during the climb.
PA.IV.C.S11	Configure the airplane after a positive rate of climb has been verified or in accordance with airplane manufacturer's instructions.
PA.IV.C.S12	Maintain V_X or V_Y, as appropriate, +10/-5 knots to a safe maneuvering altitude.
PA.IV.C.S13	Maintain directional control and proper wind-drift correction throughout takeoff and climb.
PA.IV.C.S14	Comply with noise abatement procedures.

IV. Takeoffs, Landings, and Go-Arounds

Task	D. Soft-Field Approach and Landing (ASEL)
References	FAA-H-8083-2, FAA-H-8083-3; POH/AFM; AIM
Objective	To determine that the applicant exhibits satisfactory knowledge, risk management, and skills associated with a soft-field approach and landing with emphasis on proper use and coordination of flight controls.
Knowledge	The applicant demonstrates understanding of:
PA.IV.D.K1	A stabilized approach, to include energy management concepts.
PA.IV.D.K2	Effects of atmospheric conditions, including wind, on approach and landing performance.
PA.IV.D.K3	Wind correction techniques on approach and landing.
Risk Management	The applicant demonstrates the ability to identify, assess and mitigate risks, encompassing:
PA.IV.D.R1	Selection of runway based on pilot capability, airplane performance and limitations, available distance, and wind.
PA.IV.D.R2	Effects of:
PA.IV.D.R2a	a. Crosswind
PA.IV.D.R2b	b. Windshear
PA.IV.D.R2c	c. Tailwind
PA.IV.D.R2d	d. Wake turbulence
PA.IV.D.R2e	e. Runway surface/condition
PA.IV.D.R3	Planning for:
PA.IV.D.R3a	a. Go-around and rejected landing
PA.IV.D.R3b	b. Land and hold short operations (LAHSO)
PA.IV.D.R4	Collision hazards, to include aircraft, terrain, obstacles, wires, vehicles, persons, and wildlife.
PA.IV.D.R5	Low altitude maneuvering including stall, spin, or CFIT.
PA.IV.D.R6	Distractions, loss of situational awareness, or improper task management.
Skills	The applicant demonstrates the ability to:
PA.IV.D.S1	Complete the appropriate checklist.
PA.IV.D.S2	Make radio calls as appropriate.
PA.IV.D.S3	Ensure the airplane is aligned with the correct/assigned runway.
PA.IV.D.S4	Scan the landing runway and adjoining area for traffic and obstructions.
PA.IV.D.S5	Select and aim for a suitable touchdown point considering the wind, landing surface, and obstructions.
PA.IV.D.S6	Establish the recommended approach and landing configuration and airspeed, and adjust pitch attitude and power as required to maintain a stabilized approach.
PA.IV.D.S7	Maintain manufacturer's published approach airspeed or in its absence not more than 1.3 V_{so}, +10/-5 knots with gust factor applied.
PA.IV.D.S8	Maintain directional control and appropriate crosswind correction throughout the approach and landing.
PA.IV.D.S9	Make smooth, timely, and correct control inputs during the round out and touchdown, and, for tricycle gear airplanes, keep the nose wheel off the surface until loss of elevator effectiveness.
PA.IV.D.S10	Touch down at a proper pitch attitude with minimum sink rate, no side drift, and with the airplane's longitudinal axis aligned with the center of the runway.
PA.IV.D.S11	Maintain elevator as recommended by manufacturer during rollout and exit the "soft" area at a speed that would preclude sinking into the surface.
PA.IV.D.S12	Execute a timely go-around if the approach cannot be made within the tolerances specified above or for any other condition that may result in an unsafe approach or landing.
PA.IV.D.S13	Maintain proper position of the flight controls and sufficient speed to taxi while on the soft surface.

IV. Takeoffs, Landings, and Go-Arounds

Task	E. Short-Field Takeoff and Maximum Performance Climb (ASEL, AMEL)
References	FAA-H-8083-2, FAA-H-8083-3; POH/AFM; AIM
Objective	To determine that the applicant exhibits satisfactory knowledge, risk management, and skills associated with a short-field takeoff, maximum performance climb operations, and rejected takeoff procedures.
Knowledge	The applicant demonstrates understanding of:
PA.IV.E.K1	Effects of atmospheric conditions, including wind, on takeoff and climb performance.
PA.IV.E.K2	V_X and V_Y.
PA.IV.E.K3	Appropriate airplane configuration.
Risk Management	The applicant demonstrates the ability to identify, assess and mitigate risks, encompassing:
PA.IV.E.R1	Selection of runway based on pilot capability, airplane performance and limitations, available distance, and wind.
PA.IV.E.R2	Effects of:
PA.IV.E.R2a	a. Crosswind
PA.IV.E.R2b	b. Windshear
PA.IV.E.R2c	c. Tailwind
PA.IV.E.R2d	d. Wake turbulence
PA.IV.E.R2e	e. Runway surface/condition
PA.IV.E.R3	Abnormal operations, to include planning for:
PA.IV.E.R3a	a. Rejected takeoff
PA.IV.E.R3b	b. Engine failure in takeoff/climb phase of flight
PA.IV.E.R4	Collision hazards, to include aircraft, terrain, obstacles, wires, vehicles, persons, and wildlife.
PA.IV.E.R5	Low altitude maneuvering including stall, spin, or CFIT.
PA.IV.E.R6	Distractions, loss of situational awareness, or improper task management.
Skills	The applicant demonstrates the ability to:
PA.IV.E.S1	Complete the appropriate checklist.
PA.IV.E.S2	Make radio calls as appropriate.
PA.IV.E.S3	Verify assigned/correct runway.
PA.IV.E.S4	Ascertain wind direction with or without visible wind direction indicators.
PA.IV.E.S5	Position the flight controls for the existing wind.
PA.IV.E.S6	Clear the area, taxi into takeoff position and align the airplane on the runway centerline utilizing maximum available takeoff area.
PA.IV.E.S7	Apply brakes while setting engine power to achieve maximum performance.
PA.IV.E.S8	Confirm takeoff power prior to brake release and verify proper engine and flight instrument indications prior to rotation.
PA.IV.E.S9	Rotate and lift off at the recommended airspeed and accelerate to the recommended obstacle clearance airspeed or V_X, +10/-5 knots.
PA.IV.E.S10	Establish a pitch attitude that will maintain the recommended obstacle clearance airspeed or V_X, +10/-5 knots until clearing the obstacle or until the airplane is 50 feet above the surface.
PA.IV.E.S11	Establish a pitch attitude for V_Y and accelerate to V_Y+10/-5 knots after clearing the obstacle or at 50 feet AGL if simulating an obstacle.
PA.IV.E.S12	Configure the airplane in accordance with the manufacturer's guidance after a positive rate of climb has been verified.
PA.IV.E.S13	Maintain V_Y +10/-5 knots to a safe maneuvering altitude.
PA.IV.E.S14	Maintain directional control and proper wind-drift correction throughout takeoff and climb.
PA.IV.E.S15	Comply with noise abatement procedures.

IV. Takeoffs, Landings, and Go-Arounds

Task	F. *Short-Field Approach and Landing (ASEL, AMEL)*
References	FAA-H-8083-2, FAA-H-8083-3; POH/AFM; AIM
Objective	To determine that the applicant exhibits satisfactory knowledge, risk management, and skills associated with a short-field approach and landing with emphasis on proper use and coordination of flight controls.
Knowledge	The applicant demonstrates understanding of:
PA.IV.F.K1	A stabilized approach, to include energy management concepts.
PA.IV.F.K2	Effects of atmospheric conditions, including wind, on approach and landing performance.
PA.IV.F.K3	Wind correction techniques on approach and landing.
Risk Management	The applicant demonstrates the ability to identify, assess and mitigate risks, encompassing:
PA.IV.F.R1	Selection of runway based on pilot capability, airplane performance and limitations, available distance, and wind.
PA.IV.F.R2	Effects of:
PA.IV.F.R2a	a. Crosswind
PA.IV.F.R2b	b. Windshear
PA.IV.F.R2c	c. Tailwind
PA.IV.F.R2d	d. Wake turbulence
PA.IV.F.R2e	e. Runway surface/condition
PA.IV.F.R3	Planning for:
PA.IV.F.R3a	a. Go-around and rejected landing
PA.IV.F.R3b	b. Land and hold short operations (LAHSO)
PA.IV.F.R4	Collision hazards, to include aircraft, terrain, obstacles, wires, vehicles, persons, and wildlife.
PA.IV.F.R5	Low altitude maneuvering including stall, spin, or CFIT.
PA.IV.F.R6	Distractions, loss of situational awareness, or improper task management.
Skills	The applicant demonstrates the ability to:
PA.IV.F.S1	Complete the appropriate checklist.
PA.IV.F.S2	Make radio calls as appropriate.
PA.IV.F.S3	Ensure the airplane is aligned with the correct/assigned runway.
PA.IV.F.S4	Scan the landing runway and adjoining area for traffic and obstructions.
PA.IV.F.S5	Select and aim for a suitable touchdown point considering the wind, landing surface, and obstructions.
PA.IV.F.S6	Establish the recommended approach and landing configuration and airspeed, and adjust pitch attitude and power as required to maintain a stabilized approach.
PA.IV.F.S7	Maintain manufacturer's published approach airspeed or in its absence not more than 1.3 V_{SO}, +10/-5 knots with gust factor applied.
PA.IV.F.S8	Maintain directional control and appropriate crosswind correction throughout the approach and landing.
PA.IV.F.S9	Make smooth, timely, and correct control application during the round out and touchdown.
PA.IV.F.S10	Touch down at a proper pitch attitude within 200 feet beyond or on the specified point, threshold markings, or runway numbers, with no side drift, minimum float, and with the airplane's longitudinal axis aligned with and over runway centerline.
PA.IV.F.S11	Use manufacturer's recommended procedures for airplane configuration and braking.
PA.IV.F.S12	Execute a timely go-around if the approach cannot be made within the tolerances specified above or for any other condition that may result in an unsafe approach or landing.
PA.IV.F.S13	Utilize runway incursion avoidance procedures.

IV. Takeoffs, Landings, and Go-Arounds

Task	G. *Confined Area Takeoff and Maximum Performance Climb (ASES, AMES)*
References	FAA-H-8083-2, FAA-H-8083-3, FAA-H-8083-23; POH/AFM; AIM
Objective	To determine that the applicant exhibits satisfactory knowledge, risk management, and skills associated with a confined area takeoff, and maximum performance climb operations.
Knowledge	The applicant demonstrates understanding of:
PA.IV.G.K1	Effects of atmospheric conditions, including wind, on takeoff and climb performance.
PA.IV.G.K2	V_X and V_Y.
PA.IV.G.K3	Appropriate airplane configuration.
PA.IV.G.K4	Effects of water surface.
Risk Management	The applicant demonstrates the ability to identify, assess and mitigate risks, encompassing:
PA.IV.G.R1	Selection of takeoff path based on pilot capability, airplane performance and limitations, available distance, and wind.
PA.IV.G.R2	Effects of:
PA.IV.G.R2a	a. Crosswind
PA.IV.G.R2b	b. Windshear
PA.IV.G.R2c	c. Tailwind
PA.IV.G.R2d	d. Wake turbulence
PA.IV.G.R2e	e. Water surface/condition
PA.IV.G.R3	Abnormal operations, to include planning for:
PA.IV.G.R3a	a. Rejected takeoff
PA.IV.G.R3b	b. Engine failure in takeoff/climb phase of flight
PA.IV.G.R4	Collision hazards, to include aircraft, terrain, obstacles, wires, vessels, persons, and wildlife.
PA.IV.G.R5	Low altitude maneuvering including stall, spin, or CFIT.
PA.IV.G.R6	Distractions, loss of situational awareness, or improper task management.
Skills	The applicant demonstrates the ability to:
PA.IV.G.S1	Complete the appropriate checklist.
PA.IV.G.S2	Make radio calls as appropriate.
PA.IV.G.S3	Verify assigned/correct takeoff path.
PA.IV.G.S4	Ascertain wind direction with or without visible wind direction indicators.
PA.IV.G.S5	Position the flight controls for the existing wind.
PA.IV.G.S6	Clear the area, taxi into takeoff position utilizing maximum available takeoff area and align the airplane on the takeoff path.
PA.IV.G.S7	Confirm takeoff power and proper engine and flight instrument indications prior to rotation.
PA.IV.G.S8	Establish a pitch attitude that maintains the most efficient planing/liftoff attitude and correct for porpoising and skipping.
PA.IV.G.S9	Avoid excessive water spray on the propeller(s).
PA.IV.G.S10	Rotate and liftoff at the recommended airspeed, and accelerate to the recommended obstacle clearance airspeed or V_X.
PA.IV.G.S11	Establish a pitch attitude that will maintain the recommended obstacle clearance airspeed or V_X, +10/-5 knots until the obstacle is cleared or until the airplane is 50 feet above the surface.
PA.IV.G.S12	Establish a pitch attitude for V_Y and accelerate to V_Y +10/-5 knots after clearing the obstacle or at 50 feet AGL if simulating an obstacle.
PA.IV.G.S13	Retract flaps, if extended, after a positive rate of climb has been verified or in accordance with airplane manufacturer's guidance.
PA.IV.G.S14	Maintain V_Y +10/-5 knots to a safe maneuvering altitude.
PA.IV.G.S15	Maintain directional control and proper wind-drift correction throughout takeoff and climb.
PA.IV.G.S16	Comply with noise abatement procedures.

IV. Takeoffs, Landings, and Go-Arounds

Task	H. Confined Area Approach and Landing (ASES, AMES)
References	FAA-H-8083-2, FAA-H-8083-3, FAA-H-8083-23; POH/AFM; AIM
Objective	To determine that the applicant exhibits satisfactory knowledge, risk management, and skills associated with a confined area approach and landing.
Knowledge	The applicant demonstrates understanding of:
PA.IV.H.K1	A stabilized approach, to include energy management concepts.
PA.IV.H.K2	Effects of atmospheric conditions, including wind, on approach and landing performance.
PA.IV.H.K3	Wind correction techniques on approach and landing.
Risk Management	The applicant demonstrates the ability to identify, assess and mitigate risks, encompassing:
PA.IV.H.R1	Selection of approach path and touchdown area based on pilot capability, airplane performance and limitations, available distance, and wind.
PA.IV.H.R2	Effects of:
PA.IV.H.R2a	a. Crosswind
PA.IV.H.R2b	b. Windshear
PA.IV.H.R2c	c. Tailwind
PA.IV.H.R2d	d. Wake turbulence
PA.IV.H.R2e	e. Water surface/condition
PA.IV.H.R3	Planning for a go-around and rejected landing.
PA.IV.H.R4	Collision hazards, to include aircraft, terrain, obstacles, wires, vessels, persons, and wildlife.
PA.IV.H.R5	Low altitude maneuvering including stall, spin, or CFIT.
PA.IV.H.R6	Distractions, loss of situational awareness, or improper task management.
Skills	The applicant demonstrates the ability to:
PA.IV.H.S1	Complete the appropriate checklist.
PA.IV.H.S2	Make radio calls as appropriate.
PA.IV.H.S3	Ensure the airplane is aligned for an approach to the correct/assigned landing surface.
PA.IV.H.S4	Scan the landing area for traffic and obstructions.
PA.IV.H.S5	Select and aim for a suitable touchdown point considering the wind, landing surface, and obstructions.
PA.IV.H.S6	Establish the recommended approach and landing configuration and airspeed, and adjust pitch attitude and power as required to maintain a stabilized approach.
PA.IV.H.S7	Maintain manufacturer's published approach airspeed or in its absence not more than 1.3 V_{SO}, +10/-5 knots with gust factor applied.
PA.IV.H.S8	Maintain directional control and appropriate crosswind correction throughout the approach and landing, as required.
PA.IV.H.S9	Make smooth, timely, and correct control application during the round out and touchdown.
PA.IV.H.S10	Contact the water at the recommended airspeed with a proper pitch attitude for the surface conditions.
PA.IV.H.S11	Touch down at a proper pitch attitude, within 200 feet beyond or on the specified point, with no side drift, minimum float, and with the airplane's longitudinal axis aligned with the projected landing path.
PA.IV.H.S12	Execute a timely go-around if the approach cannot be made within the tolerances specified above or for any other condition that may result in an unsafe approach or landing.
PA.IV.H.S13	Apply elevator control as necessary to stop in the shortest distance consistent with safety.

IV. Takeoffs, Landings, and Go-Arounds

Task	I. Glassy Water Takeoff and Climb (ASES, AMES)
References	FAA-H-8083-2, FAA-H-8083-23; POH/AFM; AIM
Objective	To determine that the applicant exhibits satisfactory knowledge, risk management, and skills associated with a glassy water takeoff and climb. **Note:** If a glassy water condition does not exist, the applicant must be evaluated by simulating the Task.
Knowledge	The applicant demonstrates understanding of:
PA.IV.I.K1	Effects of atmospheric conditions, including wind, on takeoff and climb performance.
PA.IV.I.K2	V_X and V_Y.
PA.IV.I.K3	Appropriate airplane configuration.
PA.IV.I.K4	Appropriate use of glassy water takeoff and climb technique.
Risk Management	The applicant demonstrates the ability to identify, assess and mitigate risks, encompassing:
PA.IV.I.R1	Selection of takeoff path based on pilot capability, airplane performance and limitations, and available distance.
PA.IV.I.R2	Water surface/condition.
PA.IV.I.R3	Abnormal operations, to include planning for:
PA.IV.I.R3a	a. Rejected takeoff
PA.IV.I.R3b	b. Engine failure in takeoff/climb phase of flight
PA.IV.I.R4	Collision hazards, to include aircraft, terrain, obstacles, wires, vessels, persons, and wildlife.
PA.IV.I.R5	Low altitude maneuvering including stall, spin, or CFIT.
PA.IV.I.R6	Distractions, loss of situational awareness, or improper task management.
PA.IV.I.R7	Failure to confirm gear position in an amphibious airplane.
Skills	The applicant demonstrates the ability to:
PA.IV.I.S1	Complete the appropriate checklist.
PA.IV.I.S2	Make radio calls as appropriate.
PA.IV.I.S3	Position flight controls and flaps for the existing conditions.
PA.IV.I.S4	Clear the area; select appropriate takeoff path considering surface hazards or vessels and surface conditions.
PA.IV.I.S5	Retract the water rudders as appropriate; advance the throttle smoothly to takeoff power.
PA.IV.I.S6	Establish and maintain an appropriate planing attitude, directional control, and correct for porpoising, skipping, and increase in water drag.
PA.IV.I.S7	Avoid excessive water spray on the propeller(s).
PA.IV.I.S8	Utilize appropriate techniques to lift seaplane from the water considering surface conditions.
PA.IV.I.S9	Establish proper attitude/airspeed and accelerate to V_Y +10/-5 knots during the climb.
PA.IV.I.S10	Configure the airplane after a positive rate of climb has been verified or in accordance with airplane manufacturer's instructions.
PA.IV.I.S11	Maintain V_Y +10/-5 knots to a safe maneuvering altitude.
PA.IV.I.S12	Maintain directional control throughout takeoff and climb.

IV. Takeoffs, Landings, and Go-Arounds

Task	J. Glassy Water Approach and Landing (ASES, AMES)
References	FAA-H-8083-2, FAA-H-8083-23; POH/AFM; AIM
Objective	To determine that the applicant exhibits satisfactory knowledge, risk management, and skills associated with a glassy water approach and landing. *Note: If a glassy water condition does not exist, the applicant must be evaluated by simulating the Task.*
Knowledge	The applicant demonstrates understanding of:
PA.IV.J.K1	A stabilized approach, to include energy management concepts.
PA.IV.J.K2	Effects of atmospheric conditions on approach and landing performance.
PA.IV.J.K3	When and why glassy water techniques are used.
PA.IV.J.K4	How a glassy water approach and landing is executed.
Risk Management	The applicant demonstrates the ability to identify, assess and mitigate risks, encompassing:
PA.IV.J.R1	Selection of approach path and touchdown area based on pilot capability, airplane performance and limitations, and available distance.
PA.IV.J.R2	Water surface/condition.
PA.IV.J.R3	Planning for go-around and rejected landing.
PA.IV.J.R4	Collision hazards, to include aircraft, terrain, obstacles, wires, vessels, persons, and wildlife.
PA.IV.J.R5	Low altitude maneuvering including stall, spin, or CFIT.
PA.IV.J.R6	Distractions, loss of situational awareness, or improper task management.
PA.IV.J.R7	Failure to confirm gear position in an amphibious airplane.
Skills	The applicant demonstrates the ability to:
PA.IV.J.S1	Complete the appropriate checklist.
PA.IV.J.S2	Make radio calls as appropriate.
PA.IV.J.S3	Scan the landing area for traffic and obstructions.
PA.IV.J.S4	Select a proper approach and landing path considering the landing surface, visual attitude references, water depth, and collision hazards.
PA.IV.J.S5	Establish the recommended approach and landing configuration and airspeed, and adjust pitch attitude and power as required to maintain a stabilized approach.
PA.IV.J.S6	Maintain manufacturer's published approach airspeed or in its absence not more than 1.3 V_{SO}, +10/-5 knots.
PA.IV.J.S7	Make smooth, timely, and correct power and control adjustments to maintain proper pitch attitude and rate of descent to touchdown.
PA.IV.J.S8	Contact the water in a proper pitch attitude, and slow to idle taxi speed.
PA.IV.J.S9	Maintain directional control throughout the approach and landing.

IV. Takeoffs, Landings, and Go-Arounds

Task	K. Rough Water Takeoff and Climb (ASES, AMES)
References	FAA-H-8083-2, FAA-H-8083-23; POH/AFM; AIM
Objective	To determine that the applicant exhibits satisfactory knowledge, risk management, and skills associated with a rough water takeoff and climb. **Note:** *If a rough water condition does not exist, the applicant must be evaluated by simulating the Task.*
Knowledge	The applicant demonstrates understanding of:
PA.IV.K.K1	Effects of atmospheric conditions, including wind, on takeoff and climb performance.
PA.IV.K.K2	V_X and V_Y.
PA.IV.K.K3	Appropriate airplane configuration.
PA.IV.K.K4	Appropriate use of rough water takeoff and climb technique.
Risk Management	The applicant demonstrates the ability to identify, assess and mitigate risks, encompassing:
PA.IV.K.R1	Selection of takeoff path based on pilot capability, airplane performance and limitations, available distance, and wind.
PA.IV.K.R2	Effects of:
PA.IV.K.R2a	a. Crosswind
PA.IV.K.R2b	b. Windshear
PA.IV.K.R2c	c. Tailwind
PA.IV.K.R2d	d. Wake turbulence
PA.IV.K.R2e	e. Water surface/condition
PA.IV.K.R3	Abnormal operations, to include planning for:
PA.IV.K.R3a	a. Rejected takeoff
PA.IV.K.R3b	b. Engine failure in takeoff/climb phase of flight
PA.IV.K.R4	Collision hazards, to include aircraft, terrain, obstacles, wires, vessels, persons, and wildlife.
PA.IV.K.R5	Low altitude maneuvering including stall, spin, or CFIT.
PA.IV.K.R6	Distractions, loss of situational awareness, or improper task management.
PA.IV.K.R7	Failure to confirm gear position in an amphibious airplane.
Skills	The applicant demonstrates the ability to:
PA.IV.K.S1	Complete the appropriate checklist.
PA.IV.K.S2	Make radio calls as appropriate.
PA.IV.K.S3	Verify assigned/correct takeoff path.
PA.IV.K.S4	Ascertain wind direction with or without visible wind direction indicators.
PA.IV.K.S5	Position flight controls and configure the airplane for the existing conditions.
PA.IV.K.S6	Clear the area, select an appropriate takeoff path considering wind, swells, surface hazards, or vessels.
PA.IV.K.S7	Retract the water rudders as appropriate; advance the throttle smoothly to takeoff power.
PA.IV.K.S8	Establish and maintain an appropriate planing attitude, directional control, and correct for porpoising, skipping, and increase in water drag.
PA.IV.K.S9	Avoid excessive water spray on the propeller(s).
PA.IV.K.S10	Lift off at minimum airspeed and accelerate to V_Y +10/- 5 knots before leaving ground effect.
PA.IV.K.S11	Configure the airplane after a positive rate of climb has been verified or in accordance with airplane manufacturer's instructions.
PA.IV.K.S12	Maintain V_Y +10/-5 knots to a safe maneuvering altitude.
PA.IV.K.S13	Maintain directional control and proper wind-drift correction throughout takeoff and climb.

IV. Takeoffs, Landings, and Go-Arounds

Task	L. Rough Water Approach and Landing (ASES, AMES)
References	FAA-H-8083-2, FAA-H-8083-23; POH/AFM; AIM
Objective	To determine that the applicant exhibits satisfactory knowledge, risk management, and skills associated with a rough water approach and landing. **Note:** If a rough water condition does not exist, the applicant must be evaluated by simulating the Task.
Knowledge	The applicant demonstrates understanding of:
PA.IV.L.K1	A stabilized approach, to include energy management concepts.
PA.IV.L.K2	Effects of atmospheric conditions, including wind, on approach and landing performance.
PA.IV.L.K3	Wind correction techniques on approach and landing.
PA.IV.L.K4	When and why rough water techniques are used.
PA.IV.L.K5	How a rough water approach and landing is executed.
Risk Management	The applicant demonstrates the ability to identify, assess and mitigate risks, encompassing:
PA.IV.L.R1	Selection of approach path and touchdown area based on pilot capability, airplane performance and limitations, available distance, and wind.
PA.IV.L.R2	Effects of:
PA.IV.L.R2a	a. Crosswind
PA.IV.L.R2b	b. Windshear
PA.IV.L.R2c	c. Tailwind
PA.IV.L.R2d	d. Wake turbulence
PA.IV.L.R2e	e. Water surface/condition
PA.IV.L.R3	Planning for go-around and rejected landing.
PA.IV.L.R4	Collision hazards, to include aircraft, terrain, obstacles, wires, vessels, persons, and wildlife.
PA.IV.L.R5	Low altitude maneuvering including stall, spin, or CFIT.
PA.IV.L.R6	Distractions, loss of situational awareness, or improper task management.
PA.IV.L.R7	Failure to confirm gear position in an amphibious airplane.
Skills	The applicant demonstrates the ability to:
PA.IV.L.S1	Complete the appropriate checklist.
PA.IV.L.S2	Make radio calls as appropriate.
PA.IV.L.S3	Ensure the airplane is aligned with the correct/assigned waterway.
PA.IV.L.S4	Scan the landing area for traffic and obstructions.
PA.IV.L.S5	Select and aim for a suitable touchdown point considering the wind, landing surface, and obstructions.
PA.IV.L.S6	Establish the recommended approach and landing configuration and airspeed, and adjust pitch attitude and power as required to maintain a stabilized approach.
PA.IV.L.S7	Maintain manufacturer's published approach airspeed or in its absence not more than 1.3 V_{SO}, +10/-5 knots with gust factor applied.
PA.IV.L.S8	Maintain directional control and appropriate crosswind correction throughout the approach and landing.
PA.IV.L.S9	Make smooth, timely, and correct power and control adjustments to maintain proper pitch attitude and rate of descent to touchdown.
PA.IV.L.S10	Contact the water in a proper pitch attitude, considering the type of rough water.

IV. Takeoffs, Landings, and Go-Arounds

Task	M. Forward Slip to a Landing (ASEL, ASES)
References	FAA-H-8083-2, FAA-H-8083-3; POH/AFM; AIM
Objective	To determine that the applicant exhibits satisfactory knowledge, risk management, and skills associated with a forward slip to a landing.
Knowledge	The applicant demonstrates understanding of:
PA.IV.M.K1	Concepts of energy management during a forward slip approach.
PA.IV.M.K2	Effects of atmospheric conditions, including wind, on approach and landing performance.
PA.IV.M.K3	Wind correction techniques during forward slip.
PA.IV.M.K4	When and why a forward slip approach is used during an approach.
Risk Management	The applicant demonstrates the ability to identify, assess and mitigate risks, encompassing:
PA.IV.M.R1	Selection of runway or approach path and touchdown area based on pilot capability, airplane performance and limitations, available distance, and wind.
PA.IV.M.R2	Effects of:
PA.IV.M.R2a	a. Crosswind
PA.IV.M.R2b	b. Windshear
PA.IV.M.R2c	c. Tailwind
PA.IV.M.R2d	d. Wake turbulence
PA.IV.M.R2e	e. Landing surface/condition
PA.IV.M.R3	Planning for:
PA.IV.M.R3a	a. Go-around and rejected landing
PA.IV.M.R3b	b. Land and hold short operations (LAHSO)
PA.IV.M.R4	Collision hazards, to include aircraft, terrain, obstacles, wires, vehicles, vessels, persons, and wildlife.
PA.IV.M.R5	Low altitude maneuvering including stall, spin, or CFIT.
PA.IV.M.R6	Distractions, loss of situational awareness, or improper task management.
PA.IV.M.R7	Forward slip operations, including fuel flowage, tail stalls with flaps, and lack of airspeed control.
PA.IV.M.R8	Surface contact with the airplane's longitudinal axis misaligned.
PA.IV.M.R9	Unstable approach.
Skills	The applicant demonstrates the ability to:
PA.IV.M.S1	Complete the appropriate checklist.
PA.IV.M.S2	Make radio calls as appropriate.
PA.IV.M.S3	Plan and follow a flightpath to the selected landing area considering altitude, wind, terrain, and obstructions.
PA.IV.M.S4	Select the most suitable touchdown point based on wind, landing surface, obstructions, and airplane limitations.
PA.IV.M.S5	Position airplane on downwind leg, parallel to landing runway.
PA.IV.M.S6	Configure the airplane correctly.
PA.IV.M.S7	As necessary, correlate crosswind with direction of forward slip and transition to sideslip before touchdown.
PA.IV.M.S8	Touch down at a proper pitch attitude, within 400 feet beyond or on the specified point, with no side drift, and with the airplane's longitudinal axis aligned with and over the runway center/landing path.
PA.IV.M.S9	Maintain a ground track aligned with the runway center/landing path.

IV. Takeoffs, Landings, and Go-Arounds

Task	N. Go-Around/Rejected Landing
References	FAA-H-8083-3, FAA-H-8083-23; POH/AFM; AIM
Objective	To determine that the applicant exhibits satisfactory knowledge, risk management, and skills associated with a go-around/rejected landing with emphasis on factors that contribute to landing conditions that may require a go-around.
Knowledge	The applicant demonstrates understanding of:
PA.IV.N.K1	A stabilized approach, to include energy management concepts.
PA.IV.N.K2	Effects of atmospheric conditions, including wind and density altitude on a go-around or rejected landing.
PA.IV.N.K3	Wind correction techniques on takeoff/departure and approach/landing.
Risk Management	The applicant demonstrates the ability to identify, assess and mitigate risks, encompassing:
PA.IV.N.R1	Delayed recognition of the need for a go-around/rejected landing.
PA.IV.N.R2	Delayed performance of a go-around at low altitude.
PA.IV.N.R3	Improper application of power.
PA.IV.N.R4	Improper airplane configuration.
PA.IV.N.R5	Collision hazards, to include aircraft, terrain, obstacles, wires, vehicles, vessels, persons, and wildlife.
PA.IV.N.R6	Low altitude maneuvering including stall, spin, or CFIT.
PA.IV.N.R7	Distractions, loss of situational awareness, or improper task management.
Skills	The applicant demonstrates the ability to:
PA.IV.N.S1	Complete the appropriate checklist.
PA.IV.N.S2	Make radio calls as appropriate.
PA.IV.N.S3	Make a timely decision to discontinue the approach to landing.
PA.IV.N.S4	Apply takeoff power immediately and transition to climb pitch attitude for V_X or V_Y as appropriate +10/-5 knots.
PA.IV.N.S5	Configure the airplane after a positive rate of climb has been verified or in accordance with airplane manufacturer's instructions.
PA.IV.N.S6	Maneuver to the side of the runway/landing area when necessary to clear and avoid conflicting traffic.
PA.IV.N.S7	Maintain V_Y +10/-5 knots to a safe maneuvering altitude.
PA.IV.N.S8	Maintain directional control and proper wind-drift correction throughout the climb.

V. Performance and Ground Reference Maneuvers

Task	A. Steep Turns
References	FAA-H-8083-2, FAA-H-8083-3; POH/AFM
Objective	To determine that the applicant exhibits satisfactory knowledge, risk management, and skills associated with steep turns. **Note:** See Appendix 7: Aircraft, Equipment, and Operational Requirements & Limitations.
Knowledge	The applicant demonstrates understanding of:
PA.V.A.K1	Purpose of steep turns.
PA.V.A.K2	Aerodynamics associated with steep turns, to include:
PA.V.A.K2a	a. Coordinated and uncoordinated flight
PA.V.A.K2b	b. Overbanking tendencies
PA.V.A.K2c	c. Maneuvering speed, including the impact of weight changes
PA.V.A.K2d	d. Load factor and accelerated stalls
PA.V.A.K2e	e. Rate and radius of turn
Risk Management	The applicant demonstrates the ability to identify, assess and mitigate risks, encompassing:
PA.V.A.R1	Failure to divide attention between airplane control and orientation.
PA.V.A.R2	Collision hazards, to include aircraft and terrain.
PA.V.A.R3	Low altitude maneuvering including stall, spin, or CFIT.
PA.V.A.R4	Distractions, improper task management, loss of situational awareness, or disorientation.
PA.V.A.R5	Failure to maintain coordinated flight.
Skills	The applicant demonstrates the ability to:
PA.V.A.S1	Clear the area.
PA.V.A.S2	Establish the manufacturer's recommended airspeed; or if one is not available, an airspeed not to exceed V_A.
PA.V.A.S3	Roll into a coordinated 360° steep turn with approximately a 45° bank.
PA.V.A.S4	Perform the Task in the opposite direction, as specified by evaluator.
PA.V.A.S5	Maintain the entry altitude ±100 feet, airspeed ±10 knots, bank ±5°, and roll out on the entry heading ±10°.

V. Performance and Ground Reference Maneuvers

Task	B. *Ground Reference Maneuvers*
References	14 CFR part 61; FAA-H-8083-2, FAA-H-8083-3
Objective	To determine that the applicant exhibits satisfactory knowledge, risk management, and skills associated with ground reference maneuvering which may include a rectangular course, S-turns, and turns around a point. ***Note:*** *See Approach 7: Aircraft, Equipment, and Operational Requirements & Limitations.*
Knowledge	The applicant demonstrates understanding of:
PA.V.B.K1	Purpose of ground reference maneuvers.
PA.V.B.K2	Effects of wind on ground track and relation to a ground reference point.
PA.V.B.K3	Effects of bank angle and groundspeed on rate and radius of turn.
PA.V.B.K4	Relationship of rectangular course to airport traffic pattern.
Risk Management	The applicant demonstrates the ability to identify, assess and mitigate risks, encompassing:
PA.V.B.R1	Failure to divide attention between airplane control and orientation.
PA.V.B.R2	Collision hazards, to include aircraft, terrain, obstacles, and wires.
PA.V.B.R3	Low altitude maneuvering including stall, spin, or CFIT.
PA.V.B.R4	Distractions, loss of situational awareness, or improper task management.
PA.V.B.R5	Failure to maintain coordinated flight.
Skills	The applicant demonstrates the ability to:
PA.V.B.S1	Clear the area.
PA.V.B.S2	Select a suitable ground reference area, line, or point as appropriate.
PA.V.B.S3	Plan the maneuver: ***Note:*** *The evaluator must select at least one maneuver for the applicant to demonstrate.*
PA.V.B.S3a	a. Rectangular course: enter a left or right pattern, 600 to 1,000 feet above ground level (AGL) at an appropriate distance from the selected reference area, 45° to the downwind leg
PA.V.B.S3b	b. S-turns: enter perpendicular to the selected reference line, 600 to 1,000 feet AGL at an appropriate distance from the selected reference area
PA.V.B.S3c	c. Turns around a point: enter at an appropriate distance from the reference point, 600 to 1,000 feet AGL at an appropriate distance from the selected reference area
PA.V.B.S4	Apply adequate wind-drift correction during straight and turning flight to maintain a constant ground track around a rectangular reference area, or to maintain a constant radius turn on each side of a selected reference line or point.
PA.V.B.S5	If performing S-Turns, reverse the turn directly over the selected reference line; if performing turns around a point, complete turns in either direction, as specified by the evaluator.
PA.V.B.S6	Divide attention between airplane control, traffic avoidance and the ground track while maintaining coordinated flight.
PA.V.B.S7	Maintain altitude ±100 feet; maintain airspeed ±10 knots.

VI. Navigation

Task	A. *Pilotage and Dead Reckoning*
References	14 CFR part 61; FAA-H-8083-2, FAA-H-8083-25; Navigation Charts
Objective	To determine that the applicant exhibits satisfactory knowledge, risk management, and skills associated with pilotage and dead reckoning.
Knowledge	The applicant demonstrates understanding of:
PA.VI.A.K1	Pilotage and dead reckoning.
PA.VI.A.K2	Magnetic compass errors.
PA.VI.A.K3	Topography.
PA.VI.A.K4	Selection of appropriate:
PA.VI.A.K4a	a. Route
PA.VI.A.K4b	b. Altitude(s)
PA.VI.A.K4c	c. Checkpoints
PA.VI.A.K5	Plotting a course, to include:
PA.VI.A.K5a	a. Determining heading, speed, and course
PA.VI.A.K5b	b. Wind correction angle
PA.VI.A.K5c	c. Estimating time, speed, and distance
PA.VI.A.K5d	d. True airspeed and density altitude
PA.VI.A.K6	Power setting selection.
PA.VI.A.K7	Planned versus actual flight plan calculations and required corrections.
Risk Management	The applicant demonstrates the ability to identify, assess and mitigate risks, encompassing:
PA.VI.A.R1	Collision hazards, to include aircraft, terrain, obstacles, and wires.
PA.VI.A.R2	Distractions, loss of situational awareness, or improper task management.
Skills	The applicant demonstrates the ability to:
PA.VI.A.S1	Prepare and use a flight log.
PA.VI.A.S2	Navigate by pilotage.
PA.VI.A.S3	Navigate by means of pre-computed headings, groundspeeds, and elapsed time.
PA.VI.A.S4	Use the magnetic direction indicator in navigation, to include turns to headings.
PA.VI.A.S5	Verify position within three nautical miles of the flight-planned route.
PA.VI.A.S6	Arrive at the en route checkpoints within five minutes of the initial or revised estimated time of arrival (ETA) and provide a destination estimate.
PA.VI.A.S7	Maintain the appropriate altitude ±200 feet and heading ±15°.

VI. Navigation

Task	B. Navigation Systems and Radar Services
References	FAA-H-8083-2, FAA-H-8083-3, FAA-H-8083-6, FAA-H-8083-25; AIM **Note:** *The evaluator should reference the manufacturer's equipment supplement(s) as necessary.*
Objective	To determine that the applicant exhibits satisfactory knowledge, risk management, and skills associated with navigation systems and radar services.
Knowledge	The applicant demonstrates understanding of:
PA.VI.B.K1	Ground-based navigation (orientation, course determination, equipment, tests, and regulations).
PA.VI.B.K2	Satellite-based navigation (e.g., equipment, regulations, database considerations, and limitations of satellite navigation).
PA.VI.B.K3	Radar assistance to VFR aircraft (e.g., operations, equipment, available services, traffic advisories).
PA.VI.B.K4	Transponder (Mode(s) A, C, and S).
Risk Management	The applicant demonstrates the ability to identify, assess and mitigate risks, encompassing:
PA.VI.B.R1	Failure to manage automated navigation and autoflight systems.
PA.VI.B.R2	Distractions, loss of situational awareness, or improper task management.
PA.VI.B.R3	Limitations of the navigation system in use.
PA.VI.B.R4	Loss of a navigation signal.
Skills	The applicant demonstrates the ability to:
PA.VI.B.S1	Use an airborne electronic navigation system.
PA.VI.B.S2	Determine the airplane's position using the navigation system.
PA.VI.B.S3	Intercept and track a given course, radial, or bearing, as appropriate.
PA.VI.B.S4	Recognize and describe the indication of station or waypoint passage, if appropriate.
PA.VI.B.S5	Recognize signal loss or interference and take appropriate action, if applicable.
PA.VI.B.S6	Use proper communication procedures when utilizing radar services.
PA.VI.B.S7	Maintain the appropriate altitude ±200 feet and heading ±15°.

VI. Navigation

Task	C. Diversion
References	FAA-H-8083-2, FAA-H-8083-25; AIM; Navigation Charts
Objective	To determine that the applicant exhibits satisfactory knowledge, risk management, and skills associated with diversion.
Knowledge	The applicant demonstrates understanding of:
PA.VI.C.K1	Selecting an alternate destination.
PA.VI.C.K2	Situations that require deviations from flight plan or ATC instructions.
Risk Management	The applicant demonstrates the ability to identify, assess and mitigate risks, encompassing:
PA.VI.C.R1	Collision hazards, to include aircraft, terrain, obstacles, and wires.
PA.VI.C.R2	Distractions, loss of situational awareness, or improper task management.
PA.VI.C.R3	Failure to make a timely decision to divert.
PA.VI.C.R4	Failure to select an appropriate airport or seaplane base.
PA.VI.C.R5	Failure to utilize all available resources (e.g., automation, ATC, and flight deck planning aids).
Skills	The applicant demonstrates the ability to:
PA.VI.C.S1	Select a suitable destination and route for diversion.
PA.VI.C.S2	Make a reasonable estimate of heading, groundspeed, arrival time, and fuel consumption to the divert airport.
PA.VI.C.S3	Maintain the appropriate altitude ±200 feet and heading ±15°.
PA.VI.C.S4	Update/interpret weather in flight.
PA.VI.C.S5	Utilize flight deck displays of digital weather and aeronautical information, as applicable.

VI. Navigation

Task	D. Lost Procedures
References	FAA-H-8083-2, FAA-H-8083-25; AIM; Navigation Charts
Objective	To determine that the applicant exhibits satisfactory knowledge, risk management, and skills associated with lost procedures and taking appropriate steps to achieve a satisfactory outcome if lost.
Knowledge	The applicant demonstrates understanding of:
PA.VI.D.K1	Methods to determine position.
PA.VI.D.K2	Assistance available if lost (e.g., radar services, communication procedures).
Risk Management	The applicant demonstrates the ability to identify, assess and mitigate risks, encompassing:
PA.VI.D.R1	Collision hazards, to include aircraft, terrain, obstacles, and wires.
PA.VI.D.R2	Distractions, loss of situational awareness, or improper task management.
PA.VI.D.R3	Failure to record times over waypoints.
PA.VI.D.R4	Failure to seek assistance or declare an emergency in a deteriorating situation.
Skills	The applicant demonstrates the ability to:
PA.VI.D.S1	Use an appropriate method to determine position.
PA.VI.D.S2	Maintain an appropriate heading and climb as necessary.
PA.VI.D.S3	Identify prominent landmarks.
PA.VI.D.S4	Use navigation systems/facilities or contact an ATC facility for assistance.

VII. Slow Flight and Stalls

Task	A. *Maneuvering During Slow Flight*
References	FAA-H-8083-2, FAA-H-8083-3, FAA-H-8083-25; POH/AFM
Objective	To determine that the applicant exhibits satisfactory knowledge, risk management, and skills associated with maneuvering during slow flight. ***Note:*** *See Appendix 6: Safety of Flight and Appendix 7: Aircraft, Equipment, and Operational Requirements & Limitations.*
Knowledge	The applicant demonstrates understanding of:
PA.VII.A.K1	Aerodynamics associated with slow flight in various airplane configurations, to include the relationship between angle of attack, airspeed, load factor, power setting, airplane weight and center of gravity, airplane attitude, and yaw effects.
Risk Management	The applicant demonstrates the ability to identify, assess and mitigate risks, encompassing:
PA.VII.A.R1	Inadvertent slow flight and flight with a stall warning, which could lead to loss of control.
PA.VII.A.R2	Range and limitations of stall warning indicators (e.g., airplane buffet, stall horn, etc.).
PA.VII.A.R3	Failure to maintain coordinated flight.
PA.VII.A.R4	Effect of environmental elements on airplane performance (e.g., turbulence, microbursts, and high-density altitude).
PA.VII.A.R5	Collision hazards, to include aircraft, terrain, obstacles, and wires.
PA.VII.A.R6	Distractions, loss of situational awareness, or improper task management.
Skills	The applicant demonstrates the ability to:
PA.VII.A.S1	Clear the area.
PA.VII.A.S2	Select an entry altitude that will allow the Task to be completed no lower than 1,500 feet AGL (ASEL, ASES) or 3,000 feet AGL (AMEL, AMES).
PA.VII.A.S3	Establish and maintain an airspeed at which any further increase in angle of attack, increase in load factor, or reduction in power, would result in a stall warning (e.g., airplane buffet, stall horn, etc.).
PA.VII.A.S4	Accomplish coordinated straight-and-level flight, turns, climbs, and descents with the airplane configured as specified by the evaluator without a stall warning (e.g., airplane buffet, stall horn, etc.).
PA.VII.A.S5	Maintain the specified altitude, ±100 feet; specified heading, ±10°; airspeed, +10/-0 knots; and specified angle of bank, ±10°.

VII. Slow Flight and Stalls

Task	B. Power-Off Stalls
References	FAA-H-8083-2, FAA-H-8083-3; AC 61-67; POH/AFM
Objective	To determine that the applicant exhibits satisfactory knowledge, risk management, and skills associated with power-off stalls. **Note:** See _Appendix 7: Aircraft, Equipment, and Operational Requirements & Limitations_.
Knowledge	The applicant demonstrates understanding of:
PA.VII.B.K1	Aerodynamics associated with stalls in various airplane configurations, to include the relationship between angle of attack, airspeed, load factor, power setting, airplane weight and center of gravity, airplane attitude, and yaw effects.
PA.VII.B.K2	Stall characteristics (i.e., airplane design) and impending stall and full stall indications (i.e., how to recognize by sight, sound, or feel).
PA.VII.B.K3	Factors and situations that can lead to a power-off stall and actions that can be taken to prevent it.
PA.VII.B.K4	Fundamentals of stall recovery.
Risk Management	The applicant demonstrates the ability to identify, assess and mitigate risks, encompassing:
PA.VII.B.R1	Factors and situations that could lead to an inadvertent power-off stall, spin, and loss of control.
PA.VII.B.R2	Range and limitations of stall warning indicators (e.g., airplane buffet, stall horn, etc.).
PA.VII.B.R3	Failure to recognize and recover at the stall warning during normal operations.
PA.VII.B.R4	Improper stall recovery procedure.
PA.VII.B.R5	Secondary stalls, accelerated stalls, and cross-control stalls.
PA.VII.B.R6	Effect of environmental elements on airplane performance related to power-off stalls (e.g., turbulence, microbursts, and high-density altitude).
PA.VII.B.R7	Collision hazards, to include aircraft, terrain, obstacles, and wires.
PA.VII.B.R8	Distractions, improper task management, loss of situational awareness, or disorientation.
Skills	The applicant demonstrates the ability to:
PA.VII.B.S1	Clear the area.
PA.VII.B.S2	Select an entry altitude that will allow the Task to be completed no lower than 1,500 feet AGL (ASEL, ASES) or 3,000 feet AGL (AMEL, AMES).
PA.VII.B.S3	Configure the airplane in the approach or landing configuration, as specified by the evaluator, and maintain coordinated flight throughout the maneuver.
PA.VII.B.S4	Establish a stabilized descent.
PA.VII.B.S5	Transition smoothly from the approach or landing attitude to a pitch attitude that will induce a stall.
PA.VII.B.S6	Maintain a specified heading ±10° if in straight flight; maintain a specified angle of bank not to exceed 20°, ±10° if in turning flight, while inducing the stall.
PA.VII.B.S7	Acknowledge cues of the impending stall and then recover promptly after a full stall occurs.
PA.VII.B.S8	Execute a stall recovery in accordance with procedures set forth in the POH/AFM.
PA.VII.B.S9	Configure the airplane as recommended by the manufacturer, and accelerate to V_X or V_Y.
PA.VII.B.S10	Return to the altitude, heading, and airspeed specified by the evaluator.

VII. Slow Flight and Stalls

Task	C. Power-On Stalls
References	FAA-H-8083-2, FAA-H-8083-3; AC 61-67; POH/AFM
Objective	To determine that the applicant exhibits satisfactory knowledge, risk management, and skills associated with power-on stalls. **Note:** See _Appendix 6: Safety of Flight_ and _Appendix 7: Aircraft, Equipment, and Operational Requirements & Limitations_.
Knowledge	The applicant demonstrates understanding of:
PA.VII.C.K1	Aerodynamics associated with stalls in various airplane configurations, to include the relationship between angle of attack, airspeed, load factor, power setting, airplane weight and center of gravity, airplane attitude, and yaw effects.
PA.VII.C.K2	Stall characteristics (i.e., airplane design) and impending stall and full stall indications (i.e., how to recognize by sight, sound, or feel).
PA.VII.C.K3	Factors and situations that can lead to a power-on stall and actions that can be taken to prevent it.
PA.VII.C.K4	Fundamentals of stall recovery.
Risk Management	The applicant demonstrates the ability to identify, assess and mitigate risks, encompassing:
PA.VII.C.R1	Factors and situations that could lead to an inadvertent power-on stall, spin, and loss of control.
PA.VII.C.R2	Range and limitations of stall warning indicators (e.g., airplane buffet, stall horn, etc.).
PA.VII.C.R3	Failure to recognize and recover at the stall warning during normal operations.
PA.VII.C.R4	Improper stall recovery procedure.
PA.VII.C.R5	Secondary stalls, accelerated stalls, elevator trim stalls, and cross-control stalls.
PA.VII.C.R6	Effect of environmental elements on airplane performance related to power-on stalls (e.g., turbulence, microbursts, and high-density altitude).
PA.VII.C.R7	Collision hazards, to include aircraft, terrain, obstacles, and wires.
PA.VII.C.R8	Distractions, improper task management, loss of situational awareness, or disorientation.
Skills	The applicant demonstrates the ability to:
PA.VII.C.S1	Clear the area.
PA.VII.C.S2	Select an entry altitude that will allow the Task to be completed no lower than 1,500 feet AGL (ASEL, ASES) or 3,000 feet AGL (AMEL, AMES).
PA.VII.C.S3	Establish the takeoff, departure, or cruise configuration, as specified by the evaluator, and maintain coordinated flight throughout the maneuver.
PA.VII.C.S4	Set power (as assigned by the evaluator) to no less than 65 percent power.
PA.VII.C.S5	Transition smoothly from the takeoff or departure attitude to the pitch attitude that will induce a stall.
PA.VII.C.S6	Maintain a specified heading ±10° if in straight flight; maintain a specified angle of bank not to exceed 20°, ±10° if in turning flight, while inducing the stall.
PA.VII.C.S7	Acknowledge cues of the impending stall and then recover promptly after a full stall occurs.
PA.VII.C.S8	Execute a stall recovery in accordance with procedures set forth in the POH/AFM.
PA.VII.C.S9	Configure the airplane as recommended by the manufacturer, and accelerate to V_X or V_Y.
PA.VII.C.S10	Return to the altitude, heading, and airspeed specified by the evaluator.

VII. Slow Flight and Stalls

Task	D. *Spin Awareness*
References	FAA-H-8083-2, FAA-H-8083-3; AC 61-67; POH/AFM
Objective	To determine that the applicant exhibits satisfactory knowledge, risk management, and skills associated with spins, flight situations where unintentional spins may occur and procedures for recovery from unintentional spins.
Knowledge	The applicant demonstrates understanding of:
PA.VII.D.K1	Aerodynamics associated with spins in various airplane configurations, to include the relationship between angle of attack, airspeed, load factor, power setting, airplane weight and center of gravity, airplane attitude, and yaw effects.
PA.VII.D.K2	What causes a spin and how to identify the entry, incipient, and developed phases of a spin.
PA.VII.D.K3	Spin recovery procedure.
Risk Management	The applicant demonstrates the ability to identify, assess and mitigate risks, encompassing:
PA.VII.D.R1	Factors and situations that could lead to inadvertent spin and loss of control.
PA.VII.D.R2	Range and limitations of stall warning indicators (e.g., airplane buffet, stall horn, etc.).
PA.VII.D.R3	Improper spin recovery procedure.
PA.VII.D.R4	Effect of environmental elements on airplane performance related to spins (e.g., turbulence, microbursts, and high-density altitude).
PA.VII.D.R5	Collision hazards, to include aircraft, terrain, obstacles, and wires.
PA.VII.D.R6	Distractions, improper task management, loss of situational awareness, or disorientation.
Skills	[Intentionally left blank]

VIII. Basic Instrument Maneuvers

Task	A. Straight-and-Level Flight
References	FAA-H-8083-2, FAA-H-8083-3, FAA-H-8083-15
Objective	To determine that the applicant exhibits satisfactory knowledge, risk management, and skills associated with flying during straight-and-level flight solely by reference to instruments.
Knowledge	The applicant demonstrates understanding of:
PA.VIII.A.K1	Flight instruments as related to:
PA.VIII.A.K1a	a. Sensitivity, limitations, and potential errors in unusual attitudes
PA.VIII.A.K1b	b. Correlation (pitch instruments/bank instruments)
PA.VIII.A.K1c	c. Function and operation
PA.VIII.A.K1d	d. Proper instrument cross-check techniques
Risk Management	The applicant demonstrates the ability to identify, assess and mitigate risks, encompassing:
PA.VIII.A.R1	Instrument flying hazards to include failure to maintain VFR, spatial disorientation, loss of control, fatigue, stress, and emergency off airport landings.
PA.VIII.A.R2	Failure to seek assistance or declare an emergency in a deteriorating situation.
PA.VIII.A.R3	Collision hazards, to include aircraft, terrain, obstacles, and wires.
PA.VIII.A.R4	Distractions, loss of situational awareness, or improper task management.
Skills	The applicant demonstrates the ability to:
PA.VIII.A.S1	Maintain straight-and-level flight using proper instrument cross-check and interpretation, and coordinated control application.
PA.VIII.A.S2	Maintain altitude ±200 feet, heading ±20°, and airspeed ±10 knots.

VIII. Basic Instrument Maneuvers

Task	B. *Constant Airspeed Climbs*
References	FAA-H-8083-2, FAA-H-8083-3, FAA-H-8083-15
Objective	To determine that the applicant exhibits satisfactory knowledge, risk management, and skills associated with attitude instrument flying during constant airspeed climbs solely by reference to instruments.
Knowledge	The applicant demonstrates understanding of:
PA.VIII.B.K1	Flight instruments as related to:
PA.VIII.B.K1a	a. Sensitivity, limitations, and potential errors in unusual attitudes
PA.VIII.B.K1b	b. Correlation (pitch instruments/bank instruments)
PA.VIII.B.K1c	c. Function and operation
PA.VIII.B.K1d	d. Proper instrument cross-check techniques
Risk Management	The applicant demonstrates the ability to identify, assess and mitigate risks, encompassing:
PA.VIII.B.R1	Instrument flying hazards to include failure to maintain VFR, spatial disorientation, loss of control, fatigue, stress, and emergency off airport landings.
PA.VIII.B.R2	Failure to seek assistance or declare an emergency in a deteriorating situation.
PA.VIII.B.R3	Collision hazards, to include aircraft, terrain, obstacles, and wires.
PA.VIII.B.R4	Distractions, loss of situational awareness, or improper task management.
Skills	The applicant demonstrates the ability to:
PA.VIII.B.S1	Transition to the climb pitch attitude and power setting on an assigned heading using proper instrument cross-check and interpretation, and coordinated flight control application.
PA.VIII.B.S2	Climb at a constant airspeed to specific altitudes in straight flight and turns.
PA.VIII.B.S3	Level off at the assigned altitude and maintain altitude ±200 feet, heading ±20°, and airspeed ±10 knots.

VIII. Basic Instrument Maneuvers

Task	C. *Constant Airspeed Descents*
References	FAA-H-8083-2, FAA-H-8083-3, FAA-H-8083-15
Objective	To determine that the applicant exhibits satisfactory knowledge, risk management, and skills associated with attitude instrument flying during constant airspeed descents solely by reference to instruments.
Knowledge	The applicant demonstrates understanding of:
PA.VIII.C.K1	Flight instruments as related to:
PA.VIII.C.K1a	a. Sensitivity, limitations, and potential errors in unusual attitudes
PA.VIII.C.K1b	b. Correlation (pitch instruments/bank instruments)
PA.VIII.C.K1c	c. Function and operation
PA.VIII.C.K1d	d. Proper instrument cross-check techniques
Risk Management	The applicant demonstrates the ability to identify, assess and mitigate risks, encompassing:
PA.VIII.C.R1	Instrument flying hazards to include failure to maintain VFR, spatial disorientation, loss of control, fatigue, stress, and emergency off airport landings.
PA.VIII.C.R2	Failure to seek assistance or declare an emergency in a deteriorating situation.
PA.VIII.C.R3	Collision hazards, to include aircraft, terrain, obstacles, and wires.
PA.VIII.C.R4	Distractions, loss of situational awareness, or improper task management.
Skills	The applicant demonstrates the ability to:
PA.VIII.C.S1	Transition to the descent pitch attitude and power setting on an assigned heading using proper instrument cross-check and interpretation, and coordinated flight control application.
PA.VIII.C.S2	Descend at a constant airspeed to specific altitudes in straight flight and turns.
PA.VIII.C.S3	Level off at the assigned altitude and maintain altitude ±200 feet, heading ±20°, and airspeed ±10 knots.

VIII. Basic Instrument Maneuvers

Task	D. *Turns to Headings*
References	FAA-H-8083-2, FAA-H-8083-3, FAA-H-8083-15
Objective	To determine that the applicant exhibits satisfactory knowledge, risk management, and skills associated with attitude instrument flying during turns to headings solely by reference to instruments.
Knowledge	The applicant demonstrates understanding of:
PA.VIII.D.K1	Flight instruments as related to:
PA.VIII.D.K1a	a. Sensitivity, limitations, and potential errors in unusual attitudes
PA.VIII.D.K1b	b. Correlation (pitch instruments/bank instruments)
PA.VIII.D.K1c	c. Function and operation
PA.VIII.D.K1d	d. Proper instrument cross-check techniques
Risk Management	The applicant demonstrates the ability to identify, assess and mitigate risks, encompassing:
PA.VIII.D.R1	Instrument flying hazards to include failure to maintain VFR, spatial disorientation, loss of control, fatigue, stress, and emergency off airport landings.
PA.VIII.D.R2	Failure to seek assistance or declare an emergency in a deteriorating situation.
PA.VIII.D.R3	Collision hazards, to include aircraft, terrain, obstacles, and wires.
PA.VIII.D.R4	Distractions, loss of situational awareness, or improper task management.
Skills	The applicant demonstrates the ability to:
PA.VIII.D.S1	Turn to headings, maintain altitude ±200 feet, maintain a standard rate turn, roll out on the assigned heading ±10°, and maintain airspeed ±10 knots.

VIII. Basic Instrument Maneuvers

Task	E. *Recovery from Unusual Flight Attitudes*
References	FAA-H-8083-2, FAA-H-8083-3, FAA-H-8083-15
Objective	To determine that the applicant exhibits satisfactory knowledge, risk management, and skills associated with attitude instrument flying while recovering from unusual attitudes solely by reference to instruments.
Knowledge	The applicant demonstrates understanding of:
PA.VIII.E.K1	Flight instruments as related to:
PA.VIII.E.K1a	a. Sensitivity, limitations, and potential errors in unusual attitudes
PA.VIII.E.K1b	b. Correlation (pitch instruments/bank instruments)
PA.VIII.E.K1c	c. Function and operation
PA.VIII.E.K1d	d. Proper instrument cross-check techniques
Risk Management	The applicant demonstrates the ability to identify, assess and mitigate risks, encompassing:
PA.VIII.E.R1	Instrument flying hazards to include failure to maintain VFR, spatial disorientation, loss of control, fatigue, stress, and emergency off airport landings.
PA.VIII.E.R2	Failure to seek assistance or declare an emergency in a deteriorating situation.
PA.VIII.E.R3	Collision hazards, to include aircraft, terrain, obstacles, and wires.
PA.VIII.E.R4	Distractions, loss of situational awareness, or improper task management.
PA.VIII.E.R5	Failure to interpret flight instruments.
PA.VIII.E.R6	Failure to unload the wings in recovering from high G situations.
PA.VII.E.R7	Exceeding the operating envelope during the recovery.
Skills	The applicant demonstrates the ability to:
PA.VIII.E.S1	Recognize unusual flight attitudes; perform the correct, coordinated, and smooth flight control application to resolve unusual pitch and bank attitudes while staying within the airplane's limitations and flight parameters.

VIII. Basic Instrument Maneuvers

Task	F. Radio Communications, Navigation Systems/Facilities, and Radar Services
References	FAA-H-8083-2, FAA-H-8083-3, FAA-H-8083-15, FAA-H-8083-25
Objective	To determine that the applicant exhibits satisfactory knowledge, risk management, and skills associated with radio communications, navigation systems/facilities, and radar services available for use during flight solely by reference to instruments.
Knowledge	The applicant demonstrates understanding of:
PA.VIII.F.K1	Operating communications equipment to include identifying and selecting radio frequencies, requesting and following ATC instructions.
PA.VIII.F.K2	Operating navigation equipment to include functions and displays, and following bearings, radials, or courses.
PA.VIII.F.K3	Air traffic control facilities and services.
Risk Management	The applicant demonstrates the ability to identify, assess and mitigate risks, encompassing:
PA.VIII.F.R1	Failure to seek assistance or declare an emergency in a deteriorating situation.
PA.VIII.F.R2	Failure to utilize all available resources (e.g., automation, ATC, and flight deck planning aids).
Skills	The applicant demonstrates the ability to:
PA.VIII.F.S1	Maintain airplane control while selecting proper communications frequencies, identifying the appropriate facility, and managing navigation equipment.
PA.VIII.F.S2	Comply with ATC instructions.
PA.VIII.F.S3	Maintain altitude ±200 feet, heading ±20°, and airspeed ±10 knots.

IX. Emergency Operations

Task	A. Emergency Descent
References	FAA-H-8083-2, FAA-H-8083-3; POH/AFM
Objective	To determine that the applicant exhibits satisfactory knowledge, risk management, and skills associated with an emergency descent. **Note:** See Appendix 6: Safety of Flight.
Knowledge	The applicant demonstrates understanding of:
PA.IX.A.K1	Situations that would require an emergency descent (e.g., depressurization, smoke, or engine fire).
PA.IX.A.K2	Immediate action items and emergency procedures.
PA.IX.A.K3	Airspeed, to include airspeed limitations.
Risk Management	The applicant demonstrates the ability to identify, assess and mitigate risks, encompassing:
PA.IX.A.R1	Failure to consider altitude, wind, terrain, obstructions, and available glide distance.
PA.IX.A.R2	Collision hazards, to include aircraft, terrain, obstacles, and wires.
PA.IX.A.R3	Improper airplane configuration.
PA.IX.A.R4	Distractions, loss of situational awareness, or improper task management.
Skills	The applicant demonstrates the ability to:
PA.IX.A.S1	Clear the area.
PA.IX.A.S2	Establish and maintain the appropriate airspeed and configuration appropriate to the scenario specified by the evaluator and as covered in POH/AFM for the emergency descent.
PA.IX.A.S3	Maintain orientation, divide attention appropriately, and plan and execute a smooth recovery.
PA.IX.A.S4	Use bank angle between 30° and 45° to maintain positive load factors during the descent.
PA.IX.A.S5	Maintain appropriate airspeed +0/-10 knots, and level off at a specified altitude ±100 feet.
PA.IX.A.S6	Complete the appropriate checklist.

IX. Emergency Operations

Task	B. *Emergency Approach and Landing (Simulated) (ASEL, ASES)*
References	FAA-H-8083-2, FAA-H-8083-3; POH/AFM
Objective	To determine that the applicant exhibits satisfactory knowledge, risk management, and skills associated with emergency approach and landing procedures. ***Note:*** *See* Appendix 6: Safety of Flight.
Knowledge	The applicant demonstrates understanding of:
PA.IX.B.K1	Immediate action items and emergency procedures.
PA.IX.B.K2	Airspeed, to include:
PA.IX.B.K2a	a. Importance of best glide speed and its relationship to distance
PA.IX.B.K2b	b. Difference between best glide speed and minimum sink speed
PA.IX.B.K2c	c. Effects of wind on glide distance
PA.IX.B.K3	Effects of atmospheric conditions on emergency approach and landing.
PA.IX.B.K4	A stabilized approach, to include energy management concepts.
PA.IX.B.K5	ELTs and other emergency locating devices.
PA.IX.B.K6	ATC services to aircraft in distress.
Risk Management	The applicant demonstrates the ability to identify, assess, and mitigate risks, encompassing:
PA.IX.B.R1	Failure to consider altitude, wind, terrain, obstructions, gliding distance, and available landing distance.
PA.IX.B.R2	Failure to plan and follow a flightpath to the selected landing area.
PA.IX.B.R3	Collision hazards, to include aircraft, terrain, obstacles, and wires.
PA.IX.B.R4	Improper airplane configuration.
PA.IX.B.R5	Low altitude maneuvering including stall, spin, or CFIT.
PA.IX.B.R6	Distractions, loss of situational awareness, or improper task management.
Skills	The applicant demonstrates the ability to:
PA.IX.B.S1	Establish and maintain the recommended best glide airspeed, ±10 knots.
PA.IX.B.S2	Configure the airplane in accordance with the POH/AFM and existing conditions.
PA.IX.B.S3	Select a suitable landing area considering altitude, wind, terrain, obstructions, and available glide distance.
PA.IX.B.S4	Plan and follow a flightpath to the selected landing area considering altitude, wind, terrain, and obstructions.
PA.IX.B.S5	Prepare for landing as specified by the evaluator.
PA.IX.B.S6	Complete the appropriate checklist.

IX. Emergency Operations

Task	C. *Systems and Equipment Malfunctions*
References	FAA-H-8083-2, FAA-H-8083-3; POH/AFM
Objective	To determine that the applicant exhibits satisfactory knowledge, risk management, and skills associated with system and equipment malfunctions appropriate to the airplane provided for the practical test and analyzing the situation and take appropriate action for simulated emergencies.
Knowledge	The applicant demonstrates understanding of:
PA.IX.C.K1	Partial or complete power loss related to the specific powerplant, including:
PA.IX.C.K1a	a. Engine roughness or overheat
PA.IX.C.K1b	b. Carburetor or induction icing
PA.IX.C.K1c	c. Loss of oil pressure
PA.IX.C.K1d	d. Fuel starvation
PA.IX.C.K2	System and equipment malfunctions specific to the airplane, including:
PA.IX.C.K2a	a. Electrical malfunction
PA.IX.C.K2b	b. Vacuum/pressure and associated flight instrument malfunctions
PA.IX.C.K2c	c. Pitot/static system malfunction
PA.IX.C.K2d	d. Electronic flight deck display malfunction
PA.IX.C.K2e	e. Landing gear or flap malfunction
PA.IX.C.K2f	f. Inoperative trim
PA.IX.C.K3	Smoke/fire/engine compartment fire.
PA.IX.C.K4	Any other system specific to the airplane (e.g., supplemental oxygen, deicing).
PA.IX.C.K5	Inadvertent door or window opening.
Risk Management	The applicant demonstrates the ability to identify, assess and mitigate risks, encompassing:
PA.IX.C.R1	Failure to use the proper checklist for a system or equipment malfunction.
PA.IX.C.R2	Distractions, loss of situational awareness, or improper task management.
Skills	The applicant demonstrates the ability to:
PA.IX.C.S1	Describe appropriate action for simulated emergencies specified by the evaluator, from at least three of the elements or sub-elements listed in K1 through K5 above.
PA.IX.C.S2	Complete the appropriate checklist.

IX. Emergency Operations

Task	D. *Emergency Equipment and Survival Gear*
References	FAA-H-8083-2, FAA-H-8083-3; POH/AFM
Objective	To determine that the applicant exhibits satisfactory knowledge, risk management, and skills associated with emergency equipment, and survival gear appropriate to the airplane and environment encountered during flight and identifying appropriate equipment that should be onboard the airplane.
Knowledge	The applicant demonstrates understanding of:
PA.IX.D.K1	Emergency Locator Transmitter (ELT) operations, limitations, and testing requirements.
PA.IX.D.K2	Fire extinguisher operations and limitations.
PA.IX.D.K3	Emergency equipment and survival gear needed for:
PA.IX.D.K3a	a. Climate extremes (hot/cold)
PA.IX.D.K3b	b. Mountainous terrain
PA.IX.D.K3c	c. Overwater operations
Risk Management	The applicant demonstrates the ability to identify, assess and mitigate risks, encompassing:
PA.IX.D.R1	Failure to plan for basic needs (water, clothing, shelter) for 48 to 72 hours.
Skills	The applicant demonstrates the ability to:
PA.IX.D.S1	Identify appropriate equipment and personal gear.
PA.IX.D.S2	Brief passengers on proper use of on-board emergency equipment and survival gear.

IX. Emergency Operations

Task	E. Engine Failure During Takeoff Before V_{MC} (Simulated) (AMEL, AMES)
References	FAA-H-8083-2, FAA-H-8083-3; FAA-P-8740-66; POH/AFM
Objective	To determine that the applicant exhibits satisfactory knowledge, risk management, and skills associated with an engine failure during takeoff before V_{MC}. **Note:** See _Appendix 6: Safety of Flight_ and _Appendix 7: Aircraft, Equipment, and Operational Requirements & Limitations_.
Knowledge	The applicant demonstrates understanding of:
PA.IX.E.K1	Factors affecting V_{MC}.
PA.IX.E.K2	V_{MC} (red line) and V_{YSE} (blue line).
PA.IX.E.K3	Accelerate/stop distance.
Risk Management	The applicant demonstrates the ability to identify, assess and mitigate risks, encompassing:
PA.IX.E.R1	Failure to plan for engine failure during takeoff.
PA.IX.E.R2	Improper airplane configuration.
PA.IX.E.R3	Distractions, loss of situational awareness, or improper task management.
Skills	The applicant demonstrates the ability to:
PA.IX.E.S1	Close the throttles smoothly and promptly when a simulated engine failure occurs.
PA.IX.E.S2	Maintain directional control and apply brakes (AMEL), or flight controls (AMES), as necessary.

IX.   Emergency Operations

Task	F. *Engine Failure After Liftoff (Simulated) (AMEL, AMES)*
References	FAA-H-8083-2, FAA-H-8083-3; FAA-P-8740-66; POH/AFM
Objective	To determine that the applicant exhibits satisfactory knowledge, risk management, and skills associated with an engine failure after liftoff. ***Note:*** See *Appendix 6: Safety of Flight* and *Appendix 7: Aircraft, Equipment, and Operational Requirements & Limitations*.
Knowledge	The applicant demonstrates understanding of:
PA.IX.F.K1	Factors affecting V_{MC}.
PA.IX.F.K2	V_{MC} (red line), V_{YSE} (blue line), and V_{SSE} (safe single-engine speed).
PA.IX.F.K3	Accelerate/stop and accelerate/go distances.
PA.IX.F.K4	How to identify, verify, feather, and secure an inoperative engine.
PA.IX.F.K5	Importance of drag reduction, to include propeller feathering, gear and flap retraction, the manufacturer's recommended control input and its relation to zero sideslip.
PA.IX.F.K6	Simulated propeller feathering and the evaluator's zero-thrust procedures and responsibilities.
Risk Management	The applicant demonstrates the ability to identify, assess and mitigate risks, encompassing:
PA.IX.F.R1	Failure to plan for engine failure after liftoff.
PA.IX.F.R2	Collision hazards, to include aircraft, terrain, obstacles, and wires.
PA.IX.F.R3	Improper airplane configuration.
PA.IX.F.R4	Low altitude maneuvering including stall, spin, or CFIT.
PA.IX.F.R5	Distractions, loss of situational awareness, or improper task management.
Skills	The applicant demonstrates the ability to:
PA.IX.F.S1	Promptly recognize an engine failure, maintain control, and utilize appropriate emergency procedures.
PA.IX.F.S2	Establish V_{YSE}; if obstructions are present, establish V_{XSE} or V_{MC} +5 knots, whichever is greater, until obstructions are cleared. Then transition to V_{YSE}.
PA.IX.F.S3	Reduce drag by retracting landing gear and flaps in accordance with the manufacturer's guidance.
PA.IX.F.S4	Simulate feathering the propeller on the inoperative engine (evaluator should then establish zero thrust on the inoperative engine).
PA.IX.F.S5	Use flight controls in the proper combination as recommended by the manufacturer, or as required to maintain best performance, and trim as required.
PA.IX.F.S6	Monitor the operating engine and make adjustments as necessary.
PA.IX.F.S7	Recognize the airplane's performance capabilities. If a climb is not possible at V_{YSE}, maintain V_{YSE} and return to the departure airport for landing, or initiate an approach to the most suitable landing area available.
PA.IX.F.S8	Simulate securing the inoperative engine.
PA.IX.F.S9	Maintain heading ±10° and airspeed ±5 knots.
PA.IX.F.S10	Complete the appropriate checklist.

IX. Emergency Operations

Task	G. Approach and Landing with an Inoperative Engine (Simulated) (AMEL, AMES)
References	FAA-H-8083-2, FAA-H-8083-3; FAA-P-8740-66; POH/AFM
Objective	To determine that the applicant exhibits satisfactory knowledge, risk management, and skills associated with an approach and landing with an engine inoperative, including engine failure on final approach. **Note:** See *Appendix 6: Safety of Flight* and *Appendix 7: Aircraft, Equipment, and Operational Requirements & Limitations.*
Knowledge	The applicant demonstrates understanding of:
PA.IX.G.K1	Factors affecting V_{MC}.
PA.IX.G.K2	V_{MC} (red line) and V_{YSE} (blue line).
PA.IX.G.K3	How to identify, verify, feather, and secure an inoperative engine.
PA.IX.G.K4	Importance of drag reduction, to include propeller feathering, gear and flap retraction, and the manufacturer's recommended flight control input and its relation to zero sideslip.
PA.IX.G.K5	Applicant responsibilities during simulated feathering.
Risk Management	The applicant demonstrates the ability to identify, assess and mitigate risks, encompassing:
PA.IX.G.R1	Failure to plan for engine failure inflight or during an approach.
PA.IX.G.R2	Collision hazards, to include aircraft, terrain, obstacles, and wires.
PA.IX.G.R3	Improper airplane configuration.
PA.IX.G.R4	Low altitude maneuvering including stall, spin, or CFIT.
PA.IX.G.R5	Distractions, loss of situational awareness, or improper task management.
PA.IX.G.R6	Possible single-engine go-around.
Skills	The applicant demonstrates the ability to:
PA.IX.G.S1	Promptly recognize an engine failure and maintain positive airplane control.
PA.IX.G.S2	Set the engine controls, reduce drag, identify and verify the inoperative engine, and simulate feathering of the propeller on the inoperative engine. (Evaluator should then establish zero thrust on the inoperative engine).
PA.IX.G.S3	Use flight controls in the proper combination as recommended by the manufacturer or as required to maintain best performance, and trim as required.
PA.IX.G.S4	Follow the manufacturer's recommended emergency procedures.
PA.IX.G.S5	Monitor the operating engine and make adjustments as necessary.
PA.IX.G.S6	Maintain the manufacturer's recommended approach airspeed +10/-5 knots, in the landing configuration with a stabilized approach, until landing is assured.
PA.IX.G.S7	Make smooth, timely, and correct control application during round out and touchdown.
PA.IX.G.S8	Touch down on the first one-third of available runway/landing surface, with no drift, and the airplane's longitudinal axis aligned with and over the runway center or landing path.
PA.IX.G.S9	Maintain directional control and appropriate crosswind correction throughout the approach and landing.
PA.IX.G.S10	Complete the appropriate checklist.

X. Multiengine Operations

Task	A. Maneuvering with One Engine Inoperative (AMEL, AMES)
References	FAA-H-8083-2, FAA-H-8083-3; FAA-P-8740-66; POH/AFM
Objective	To determine that the applicant exhibits satisfactory knowledge, risk management, and skills associated with maneuvering with one engine inoperative. **Note:** See _Appendix 6: Safety of Flight_ and _Appendix 7: Aircraft, Equipment, and Operational Requirements & Limitations_.
Knowledge	The applicant demonstrates understanding of:
PA.X.A.K1	Factors affecting V_{MC}.
PA.X.A.K2	V_{MC} (red line) and V_{YSE} (blue line).
PA.X.A.K3	How to identify, verify, feather, and secure an inoperative engine.
PA.X.A.K4	Importance of drag reduction, to include propeller feathering, gear and flap retraction, the manufacturer's recommended flight control input and its relation to zero sideslip.
PA.X.A.K5	Feathering, securing, unfeathering, and restarting.
Risk Management	The applicant demonstrates the ability to identify, assess and mitigate risks, encompassing:
PA.X.A.R1	Failure to plan for engine failure during flight.
PA.X.A.R2	Collision hazards, to include aircraft, terrain, obstacles, and wires.
PA.X.A.R3	Improper airplane configuration.
PA.X.A.R4	Low altitude maneuvering including stall, spin, or CFIT.
PA.X.A.R5	Distractions, loss of situational awareness, or improper task management.
Skills	The applicant demonstrates the ability to:
PA.X.A.S1	Recognize an engine failure, maintain control, use manufacturer's memory item procedures, and utilize appropriate emergency procedures.
PA.X.A.S2	Set the engine controls, identify and verify the inoperative engine, and feather the appropriate propeller.
PA.X.A.S3	Use flight controls in the proper combination as recommended by the manufacturer, or as required to maintain best performance, and trim as required.
PA.X.A.S4	Attempt to determine and resolve the reason for the engine failure.
PA.X.A.S5	Secure the inoperative engine and monitor the operating engine and make necessary adjustments.
PA.X.A.S6	Restart the inoperative engine using manufacturer's restart procedures.
PA.X.A.S7	Maintain altitude ±100 feet or a minimum sink rate if applicable, airspeed ±10 knots, and headings ±10°.
PA.X.A.S8	Complete the appropriate checklist.

X. Multiengine Operations

Task	B. V_{MC} Demonstration (AMEL, AMES)
References	FAA-H-8083-2, FAA-H-8083-3; FAA-P-8740-66; POH/AFM
Objective	To determine that the applicant exhibits satisfactory knowledge, risk management, and skills associated with a V_{MC} demonstration. **Note:** See _Appendix 6: Safety of Flight_ and _Appendix 7: Aircraft, Equipment, and Operational Requirements & Limitations_.
Knowledge	The applicant demonstrates understanding of:
PA.X.B.K1	Factors affecting V_{MC} and how V_{MC} differs from stall speed (V_S).
PA.X.B.K2	V_{MC} (red line), V_{YSE} (blue line), and V_{SSE} (safe single-engine speed).
PA.X.B.K3	Cause of loss of directional control at airspeeds below V_{MC}.
PA.X.B.K4	Proper procedures for maneuver entry and safe recovery.
Risk Management	The applicant demonstrates the ability to identify, assess and mitigate risks, encompassing:
PA.X.B.R1	Improper airplane configuration.
PA.X.B.R2	Maneuvering with one engine inoperative.
PA.X.B.R3	Distractions, loss of situational awareness, or improper task management.
Skills	The applicant demonstrates the ability to:
PA.X.B.S1	Configure the airplane in accordance with the manufacturer's recommendations, in the absence of the manufacturer's recommendations, then at V_{SSE}/V_{YSE}, as appropriate, and:
PA.X.B.S1a	a. Landing gear retracted
PA.X.B.S1b	b. Flaps set for takeoff
PA.X.B.S1c	c. Cowl flaps set for takeoff
PA.X.B.S1d	d. Trim set for takeoff
PA.X.B.S1e	e. Propellers set for high RPM
PA.X.B.S1f	f. Power on critical engine reduced to idle and propeller windmilling
PA.X.B.S1g	g. Power on operating engine set to takeoff or maximum available power
PA.X.B.S2	Establish a single-engine climb attitude with the airspeed at approximately 10 knots above V_{SSE}.
PA.X.B.S3	Establish a bank angle not to exceed 5° toward the operating engine, as required for best performance and controllability.
PA.X.B.S4	Increase the pitch attitude slowly to reduce the airspeed at approximately 1 knot per second while applying rudder pressure to maintain directional control until full rudder is applied.
PA.X.B.S5	Recognize indications of loss of directional control, stall warning, or buffet.
PA.X.B.S6	Recover promptly by simultaneously reducing power sufficiently on the operating engine, decreasing the angle of attack as necessary to regain airspeed and directional control, and without adding power on the simulated failed engine.
PA.X.B.S7	Recover within 20° of entry heading.
PA.X.B.S8	Advance power smoothly on the operating engine and accelerate to V_{SSE}/V_{YSE}, as appropriate, +10/-5 knots during recovery.

X. Multiengine Operations

Task	**C. One Engine Inoperative (Simulated) (solely by Reference to Instruments) During Straight-and-Level Flight and Turns (AMEL, AMES)**
References	FAA-H-8083-2, FAA-H-8083-3; FAA-P-8740-66; POH/AFM
Objective	To determine that the applicant exhibits satisfactory knowledge, risk management, and skills associated with flight solely by reference to instruments with one engine inoperative. **Note:** See *Appendix 6: Safety of Flight* and *Appendix 7: Aircraft, Equipment, and Operational Requirements & Limitations*.
Knowledge	The applicant demonstrates understanding of:
PA.X.C.K1	Procedures used if engine failure occurs during straight-and-level flight and turns while on instruments.
Risk Management	The applicant demonstrates the ability to identify, assess and mitigate risks, encompassing:
PA.X.C.R1	Failure to identify the inoperative engine.
PA.X.C.R2	Inability to climb or maintain altitude with an inoperative engine.
PA.X.C.R3	Low altitude maneuvering including stall, spin, or CFIT.
PA.X.C.R4	Distractions, loss of situational awareness, or improper task management.
PA.X.C.R5	Fuel management during single-engine operation.
Skills	The applicant demonstrates the ability to:
PA.X.C.S1	Promptly recognize an engine failure and maintain positive airplane control.
PA.X.C.S2	Set the engine controls, reduce drag, identify and verify the inoperative engine, and simulate feathering of the propeller on the inoperative engine. (Evaluator should then establish zero thrust on the inoperative engine.)
PA.X.C.S3	Establish the best engine-inoperative airspeed and trim the airplane.
PA.X.C.S4	Use flight controls in the proper combination as recommended by the manufacturer, or as required to maintain best performance, and trim as required.
PA.X.C.S5	Verify the prescribed checklist procedures normally used for securing the inoperative engine.
PA.X.C.S6	Attempt to determine and resolve the reason for the engine failure.
PA.X.C.S7	Monitor engine functions and make necessary adjustments.
PA.X.C.S8	Maintain the specified altitude ±100 feet or minimum sink rate if applicable, airspeed ±10 knots, and the specified heading ±10°.
PA.X.C.S9	Assess the airplane's performance capability and decide an appropriate action to ensure a safe landing.
PA.X.C.S10	Avoid loss of airplane control or attempted flight contrary to the engine-inoperative operating limitations of the airplane.
PA.X.C.S11	Utilize SRM.

X. Multiengine Operations

Task	D. *Instrument Approach and Landing with an Inoperative Engine (Simulated) (solely by Reference to Instruments) (AMEL, AMES)*
References	FAA-H-8083-2, FAA-H-8083-3; FAA-P-8740-66; POH/AFM
Objective	To determine that the applicant exhibits satisfactory knowledge, risk management, and skills associated with executing a published instrument approach solely by reference to instruments with one engine inoperative. ***Note:*** *See Appendix 6: Safety of Flight and Appendix 7: Aircraft, Equipment, and Operational Requirements & Limitations.*
Knowledge	The applicant demonstrates understanding of:
PA.X.D.K1	Instrument approach procedures with one engine inoperative.
Risk Management	The applicant demonstrates the ability to identify, assess, and mitigate risks, encompassing:
PA.X.D.R1	Failure to plan for engine failure during approach and landing.
PA.X.D.R2	Collision hazards, to include aircraft, terrain, obstacles, wires, vehicles, vessels, persons, and wildlife.
PA.X.D.R3	Improper airplane configuration.
PA.X.D.R4	Low altitude maneuvering including stall, spin, or CFIT.
PA.X.D.R5	Distractions, loss of situational awareness, or improper task management.
PA.X.D.R6	Performing a go-around/rejected landing with an engine failure.
Skills	The applicant demonstrates the ability to:
PA.X.D.S1	Promptly recognize engine failure and maintain positive airplane control.
PA.X.D.S2	Set the engine controls, reduce drag, identify and verify the inoperative engine, and simulate feathering of the propeller on the inoperative engine. (Evaluator should then establish zero thrust on the inoperative engine).
PA.X.D.S3	Use flight controls in the proper combination as recommended by the manufacturer, or as required to maintain best performance, and trim as required.
PA.X.D.S4	Follow the manufacturer's recommended emergency procedures.
PA.X.D.S5	Monitor the operating engine and make adjustments as necessary.
PA.X.D.S6	Request and follow an actual or a simulated ATC clearance for an instrument approach.
PA.X.D.S7	Maintain altitude ±100 feet or minimum sink rate if applicable, airspeed ±10 knots, and selected heading ±10°.
PA.X.D.S8	Establish a rate of descent that will ensure arrival at the MDA or DA/DH with the airplane in a position from which a descent to a landing on the intended runway can be made, either straight in or circling as appropriate.
PA.X.D.S9	On final approach segment, maintain vertical (as applicable) and lateral guidance within ¾-scale deflection.
PA.X.D.S10	Avoid loss of airplane control, or attempted flight contrary to the operating limitations of the airplane.
PA.X.D.S11	Comply with the published criteria for the aircraft approach category if circling.
PA.X.D.S12	Execute a normal landing.
PA.X.D.S13	Complete the appropriate checklist.

XI. Night Operations

Task	A. Night Preparation
References	FAA-H-8083-2, FAA-H-8083-3, FAA-H-8083-25; AIM; POH/AFM
Objective	To determine that the applicant exhibits satisfactory knowledge, risk management, and skills associated with night operations.
Knowledge	The applicant demonstrates understanding of:
PA.XI.A.K1	Physiological aspects of vision related to night flying.
PA.XI.A.K2	Lighting systems identifying airports, runways, taxiways and obstructions, as well as pilot controlled lighting.
PA.XI.A.K3	Airplane equipment and lighting requirements for night operations.
PA.XI.A.K4	Personal equipment essential for night flight.
PA.XI.A.K5	Night orientation, navigation, and chart reading techniques.
Risk Management	The applicant demonstrates the ability to identify, assess and mitigate risks, encompassing:
PA.XI.A.R1	Collision hazards, to include aircraft, terrain, obstacles, and wires.
PA.XI.A.R2	Distractions, loss of situational awareness, or improper task management.
PA.XI.A.R3	Hazards specific to night flying.
Skills	*N/A* ***Note:*** *Not generally evaluated in flight. If the practical test is conducted at night, all ACS Tasks are evaluated in that environment, thus there is no need for explicit Task elements to exist here.*

XII. Postflight Procedures

Task	A. After Landing, Parking and Securing (ASEL, AMEL)
References	FAA-H-8083-2, FAA-H-8083-3; POH/AFM
Objective	To determine that the applicant exhibits satisfactory knowledge, risk management, and skills associated with after landing, parking, and securing procedures.
Knowledge	The applicant demonstrates understanding of:
PA.XII.A.K1	Airplane shutdown, securing, and postflight inspection.
PA.XII.A.K2	Documenting in-flight/postflight discrepancies.
Risk Management	The applicant demonstrates the ability to identify, assess and mitigate risks, encompassing:
PA.XII.A.R1	Inappropriate activities and distractions.
PA.XII.A.R2	Confirmation or expectation bias as related to taxi instructions.
PA.XII.A.R3	Airport specific security procedures.
PA.XII.A.R4	Disembarking passengers.
Skills	The applicant demonstrates the ability to:
PA.XII.A.S1	Utilize runway incursion avoidance procedures.
PA.XII.A.S2	Park in an appropriate area, considering the safety of nearby persons and property.
PA.XII.A.S3	Complete the appropriate checklist.
PA.XII.A.S4	Conduct a postflight inspection and document discrepancies and servicing requirements, if any.
PA.XII.A.S5	Secure the airplane.

XII. Postflight Procedures

Task	B. Seaplane Post-Landing Procedures (ASES, AMES)
References	FAA-H-8083-2, FAA-H-8083-23; POH/AFM
Objective	To determine that the applicant exhibits satisfactory knowledge, risk management, and skills associated with anchoring, docking, mooring, and ramping/beaching. **Note:** *The evaluator must select at least one after-landing procedure (anchoring, docking and mooring, or ramping/beaching).*
Knowledge	The applicant demonstrates understanding of:
PA.XII.B.K1	Mooring.
PA.XII.B.K2	Docking.
PA.XII.B.K3	Anchoring.
PA.XII.B.K4	Beaching/ramping.
PA.XII.B.K5	Postflight inspection, recording of in-flight/postflight discrepancies.
Risk Management	The applicant demonstrates the ability to identify, assess and mitigate risks, encompassing:
PA.XII.B.R1	Inappropriate activities and distractions.
PA.XII.B.R2	Confirmation or expectation bias as related to taxi instructions.
PA.XII.B.R3	Seaplane base specific security procedures, if applicable.
PA.XII.B.R4	Disembarking passengers.
Skills	The applicant demonstrates the ability to:
PA.XII.B.S1	If anchoring, select a suitable area considering seaplane movement, water depth, tide, wind, and weather changes. Use an adequate number of anchors and lines of sufficient strength and length to ensure the seaplane's security.
PA.XII.B.S2	If not anchoring, approach the dock/mooring buoy or beach/ramp in the proper direction and at a safe speed, considering water depth, tide, current, and wind.
PA.XII.B.S3	Complete the appropriate checklist.
PA.XII.B.S4	Conduct a postflight inspection and document discrepancies and servicing requirements, if any.
PA.XII.B.S5	Secure the seaplane considering the effect of wind, waves, and changes in water level, or comply with applicable after landing, parking and securing if operating an amphibious airplane on land.

Appendix Table of Contents

Appendix 1: The Knowledge Test Eligibility, Prerequisites, and Testing Centers A-1

    Knowledge Test Description A-1

    Knowledge Test Table A-1

    Knowledge Test Blueprint A-1

    English Language Standard A-2

    Knowledge Test Requirements A-2

    Knowledge Test Centers A-2

    Knowledge Test Registration A-2

Appendix 2: Knowledge Test Procedures and Tips A-3

    Acceptable Materials A-3

    Test Tips A-3

    Cheating or Other Unauthorized Conduct A-4

    Testing Procedures for Applicants Requesting Special Accommodations A-4

Appendix 3: Airman Knowledge Test Report A-5

    FAA Knowledge Test Question Coding A-5

    Applicant Name Considerations for the Airman Knowledge Test Report (AKTR) and the Practical
    Test Application Form A-6

Appendix 4: The Practical Test – Eligibility and Prerequisites A-7

Appendix 5: Practical Test Roles, Responsibilities, and Outcomes A-8

    Applicant Responsibilities A-8

    Instructor Responsibilities A-8

    Evaluator Responsibilities A-8

    Possible Outcomes of the Test A-9

        Satisfactory Performance A-9

        Unsatisfactory Performance A-9

        Discontinuance A-10

        Testing after Discontinuance or Unsatisfactory Performance A-10

    Additional Rating Task Table A-12

    Removal of the "Airplane Multiengine VFR Only" Limitation A-16

    Removal of the "Limited to Center Thrust" Limitation A-16

Appendix 6: Safety of Flight A-17

    General A-17

    Stall and Spin Awareness A-17

    Use of Checklists A-17

    Use of Distractions A-17

    Positive Exchange of Flight Controls A-17

    Aeronautical Decision-Making, Risk Management, Crew Resource Management and Single-Pilot
    Resource Management A-17

    Multiengine Considerations A-18

    Single-Engine Considerations A-18

High-Performance Airplane Considerations A-18

Appendix 7: Aircraft, Equipment, and Operational Requirements & Limitations A-19

Aircraft Requirements & Limitations A-19

Equipment Requirements & Limitations A-19

Operational Requirements, Limitations, & Task Information A-19

Appendix 8: Use of Flight Simulation Training Devices (FSTD) and Aviation Training Devices (ATD): Airplane Single-Engine, Multiengine Land and Sea A-21

Use of Flight Simulator Training Devices A-21

Use of Aviation Training Devices A-21

Credit for Time in an FSTD A-22

Credit for Time in an ATD A-22

Use of an FSTD on a Practical Test A-23

Appendix 9: References A-24

Appendix 10: Abbreviations and Acronyms... A-25

Appendix 1: The Knowledge Test Eligibility, Prerequisites, and Testing Centers

Knowledge Test Description

The knowledge test is an important part of the airman certification process. Applicants must pass the knowledge test before taking the practical test.

The knowledge test consists of objective, multiple-choice questions. There is a single correct response for each test question. Each test question is independent of other questions. A correct response to one question does not depend upon, or influence, the correct response to another.

Knowledge Test Table

Test Code	Test Name	Number of Questions	Age	Allotted Time	Passing Score
PAR	Private Pilot Airplane	60	15	2.5	70
PAT	Private Pilot Airplane/Recreational Pilot - Transition	30	15	1.5	70
PBG	Private Pilot Balloon - Gas	60	14	2.5	70
PBH	Private Pilot Balloon - Hot Air	60	14	2.5	70
PCH	Private Pilot Helicopter *Canadian Conversion*	40	16	2.0	70
PCP	Private Pilot – Airplane *Canadian Conversion*	40	16	2.0	70
PGL	Private Pilot Glider	60	14	2.5	70
PGT	Private Pilot Gyroplane/Recreational Pilot - Transition	30	15	1.5	70
PHT	Private Pilot Helicopter/Recreational Pilot - Transition	30	15	1.5	70
PLA	Private Pilot Airship	60	15	2.5	70
PPP	Private Pilot Powered Parachute	60	15	2.5	70
PRG	Private Pilot Gyroplane	60	15	2.5	70
PRH	Private Pilot Helicopter	60	15	2.5	70
PWS	Private Pilot Weight-Shift-Control	60	15	2.5	70

Knowledge Test Blueprint

PAR Knowledge Areas Required by 14 CFR part 61, section 61.105 to be on the Knowledge Test	Percent of Questions Per Test
Regulations	5 – 15%
Accident Reporting	5 – 10%
Performance Charts	5 – 10%
Radio Communications	5 – 10%
Weather	5 – 10%
Safe and Efficient Operations	5 – 15%
Density Altitude Performance	5 – 10%
Weight and Balance	5 – 10%
Aerodynamics, Powerplants, and Aircraft Systems	5 – 10%
Stalls and Spins	5 – 10%
Aeronautical Decision-Making (ADM)	5 – 10%
Preflight actions	5 – 10%
Total Number of Questions	**60**

English Language Standard

In accordance with the requirements of 14 CFR part 61, section 61.13(c) the applicant must demonstrate the ability to read, write, speak, and understand the English language throughout the application and testing process. English language proficiency is required to communicate effectively with Air Traffic Control (ATC), to comply with ATC instructions, and to ensure clear and effective crew communication and coordination. Normal restatement of questions as would be done for a native English speaker is permitted, and does not constitute grounds for disqualification. The FAA Aviation English Language Standard (AELS) is the FAA evaluator's benchmark. It requires the applicant to demonstrate at least the International Civil Aviation Organization (ICAO) level 4 standard.

Knowledge Test Requirements

In order to take the Private Pilot Knowledge Test, you must provide proper identification. To verify your eligibility to take the test, you must also provide one of the following in accordance with the requirements of 14 CFR part 61:

- 14 CFR part 61, section 61.35 lists the prerequisites for taking the knowledge test, to include the minimum age an applicant must be to take the test.

    Received an endorsement, if required by this part, from an authorized instructor certifying that the applicant accomplished the appropriate ground-training or a home-study course required by this part for the certificate or rating sought and is prepared for the knowledge test;

    Proper identification at the time of application that contains the applicant's—

    - (i) Photograph;
    - (ii) Signature;
    - (iii) Date of birth; and
    - (iv) Physical, residential address.

- 14 CFR part 61, section 61.49 acceptable forms of retest authorization for **all** Private Pilot tests:

    An applicant retesting **after failure** is required to submit the applicable Airman Knowledge Test Report indicating failure, along with an endorsement from an authorized instructor who gave the applicant the required additional training. The endorsement must certify that the applicant is competent to pass the test. The test proctor must retain the original failed Airman Knowledge Test Report presented as authorization and attach it to the applicable sign-in/out log.

    Note: *If the applicant no longer possesses the original Airman Knowledge Test Report, he or she may request a duplicate replacement issued by the Airmen Certification Branch.*

- Acceptable forms of authorization for Private Pilot Canadian Conversion (PCP) only:

    Confirmation of Verification Letter issued by the Office of Foundational Business, Civil Aviation Division, Airmen Certification Branch (Knowledge Testing Authorization Requirements Matrix).

    Requires **no** instructor endorsement or other form of written authorization.

Knowledge Test Centers

The FAA authorizes hundreds of knowledge testing center locations that offer a full range of airman knowledge tests. For information on authorized testing centers and to register for the knowledge test, contact one of the providers listed at www.faa.gov.

Knowledge Test Registration

When you contact a knowledge testing center to register for a test, please be prepared to select a test date, choose a testing center, and make financial arrangements for test payment when you call. You may register for test(s) several weeks in advance, and you may cancel in accordance with the testing center's cancellation policy.

Appendix 2: Knowledge Test Procedures and Tips

Before starting the actual test, the testing center will provide an opportunity to practice navigating through the test. This practice or tutorial session may include sample questions to familiarize the applicant with the look and feel of the software. (e.g., selecting an answer, marking a question for later review, monitoring time remaining for the test, and other features of the testing software.)

Acceptable Materials

The applicant may use the following aids, reference materials, and test materials, as long as the material does not include actual test questions or answers:

Acceptable Materials	Unacceptable Materials	Notes
Supplement book provided by proctor	Written materials that are handwritten, printed, or electronic	Testing centers may provide calculators and/or deny the use of personal calculators
All models of aviation-oriented calculators or small electronic calculators that perform only arithmetic functions	Electronic calculators incorporating permanent or continuous type memory circuits without erasure capability	Unit Member (proctor) may prohibit the use of your calculator if he or she is unable to determine the calculator's erasure capability
Calculators with simple programmable memories, which allow addition to, subtraction from, or retrieval of one number from the memory; or simple functions, such as square root and percentages	Magnetic Cards, magnetic tapes, modules, computer chips, or any other device upon which pre-written programs or information related to the test can be stored and retrieved	Printouts of data must be surrendered at the completion of the test if the calculator incorporates this design feature
Scales, straightedges, protractors, plotters, navigation computers, blank log sheets, holding pattern entry aids, and electronic or mechanical calculators that are directly related to the test	Dictionaries	Before, and upon completion of the test, while in the presence of the Unit Member, actuate the ON/OFF switch or RESET button, and perform any other function that ensures erasure of any data stored in memory circuits
Manufacturer's permanently inscribed instructions on the front and back of such aids, e.g., formulas, conversions, regulations, signals, weather data, holding pattern diagrams, frequencies, weight and balance formulas, and air traffic control procedures	Any booklet or manual containing instructions related to use of test aids	Unit Member makes the final determination regarding aids, reference materials, and test materials

Test Tips

When taking a knowledge test, please keep the following points in mind:

- Carefully read the instructions provided with the test.
- Answer each question in accordance with the latest regulations and guidance publications.
- Read each question carefully before looking at the answer options. You should clearly understand the problem before trying to solve it.
- After formulating a response, determine which answer option corresponds with your answer. The answer you choose should completely solve the problem.
- Remember that only one answer is complete and correct. The other possible answers are either incomplete or erroneous.

A-3

- If a certain question is difficult for you, mark it for review and return to it after you have answered the less difficult questions. This procedure will enable you to use the available time to maximum advantage.
- When solving a calculation problem, be sure to read all the associated notes.
- For questions involving use of a graph, you may request a printed copy that you can mark in computing your answer. This copy and all other notes and paperwork must be given to the testing center upon completion of the test.

Cheating or Other Unauthorized Conduct

To avoid test compromise, computer testing centers must follow strict security procedures established by the FAA and described in FAA Order 8080.6 (as amended), Conduct of Airman Knowledge Tests. The FAA has directed testing centers to terminate a test at any time a test unit member suspects that a cheating incident has occurred.

The FAA will investigate and, if the agency determines that cheating or unauthorized conduct has occurred, any airman certificate or rating you hold may be revoked. You will also be prohibited from applying for or taking any test for a certificate or rating under 14 CFR part 61 for a period of 1 year.

Testing Procedures for Applicants Requesting Special Accommodations

An applicant with learning or reading disability may request approval from the Airman Testing Branch through the local Flight Standards District Office (FSDO) or International Field Office/International Field Unit (IFO/IFU) to take airman knowledge test using one of the three options listed below, in preferential order:

Option 1: Use current testing facilities and procedures whenever possible.

Option 2: Use a self-contained, electronic device, which pronounces and displays typed-in words (e.g., the Franklin Speaking Wordmaster®) to facilitate the testing process.

> **Note:** *The device should consist of an electronic thesaurus that audibly pronounces typed-in words and presents them on a display screen. The device should also have a built-in headphone jack in order to avoid disturbing others during testing.*

Option 3: Request the proctor's assistance in reading specific words or terms from the test questions and/or supplement book. To prevent compromising the testing process, the proctor must be an individual with no aviation background or expertise. The proctor may provide reading assistance only (i.e., no explanation of words or terms). When an applicant requests this option, the FSDO or IFO/IFU inspector must contact the Airman Testing Branch for assistance in selecting the test site and assisting the proctor. Before approving any option, the FSDO or IFO/IFU inspector must advise the applicant of the regulatory certification requirement to be able to read, write, speak, and understand the English language.

Appendix 3: Airman Knowledge Test Report

Immediately upon completion of the knowledge test, the applicant receives a printed Airman Knowledge Test Report (AKTR) documenting the score with the testing center's raised, embossed seal. The applicant must retain the original AKTR. The instructor must provide instruction in each area of deficiency and provide a logbook endorsement certifying that the applicant has demonstrated satisfactory knowledge in each area. When taking the practical test, the applicant must present the original AKTR to the evaluator, who is required to assess the noted areas of deficiency during the ground portion of the practical test.

An AKTR expires 24 calendar months after the month the applicant completes the knowledge test. If the AKTR expires before completion of the practical test, the applicant must retake the knowledge test.

To obtain a duplicate AKTR due to loss or destruction of the original, the applicant can send a signed request accompanied by a check or money order for $12.00 (U.S. funds), payable to the FAA to the following address:

> Federal Aviation Administration
> Airmen Certification Branch
> P.O. Box 25082
> Oklahoma City, OK 73125

To obtain a copy of the application form or a list of the information required, please see the Airmen Certification Branch webpage.

FAA Knowledge Test Question Coding

Each Task in the ACS includes an ACS code. This ACS code will ultimately be displayed on the AKTR to indicate what Task element was proven deficient on the knowledge test. Instructors can then provide remedial training in the deficient areas, and evaluators can re-test this element during the practical test.

The ACS coding consists of four elements. For example, this code is interpreted as follows:

PA.XI.A.K1:

PA	=	Applicable ACS (Private Pilot – Airplane)
XI	=	Area of Operation (Night Operations)
A	=	Task (Night Preparation)
K1	=	Task element Knowledge 1 (Physiological aspects of vision related to night flying.)

Knowledge test questions correspond to the ACS codes, which will ultimately replace the system of Learning Statement Codes (LSC). After this transition occurs, the AKTR will list an ACS code that correlates to a specific Task element for a given Area of Operation and Task. Remedial instruction and re-testing will be specific, targeted, and based on specified learning criteria. Similarly, a Notice of Disapproval for the practical test will use the ACS codes to identify the deficient Task elements. Applicants and evaluators should interpret the codes using the ACS revision in effect on the date of the knowledge test

However, for knowledge tests taken before this system comes on line, only the LSC code (e.g., "PLT058") will be displayed on the AKTR. The LSC codes link to references and broad subject areas. By contrast, each ACS code represents a unique Task element in the ACS. Because of this fundamental difference, there is no one-to-one correlation between Learning Statement (PLT) codes and ACS codes.

Because all active knowledge test questions for the Private Pilot Airplane Knowledge Test (PAR) now align with this ACS, evaluators can use LSC codes in conjunction with this ACS for targeted retesting of missed knowledge subject areas. The evaluator should look up the LSC code(s) on the applicant's AKTR in the Learning Statement Reference Guide. After noting the subject area(s), the evaluator can use the corresponding Area(s) of Operation/Task(s) in the ACS to narrow the scope of material for retesting to the appropriate ACS Area(s) of Operation and Task(s). Evaluators must verify the applicant has sufficient knowledge in those areas associated with incorrect responses on the knowledge test.

Applicant Name Considerations for the Airman Knowledge Test Report (AKTR) and the Practical Test Application Form

The applicant uses his or her full legal name on the Airman Certificate and/or Rating Application, FAA Form 8710-1, using up to 50 characters (including spaces). The applicant may exclude some middle names as necessary to meet the 50-character limit. The AKTR may not reflect the applicant's full legal name and may differ slightly from the name presented for the practical test.

If the 8710-1 shows a middle name, the AKTR may show that middle name, the correct middle initial, or no entry. The application will process correctly using the Integrated Airman Certificate and Rating Application (IACRA) system, and the Airmen Certification Branch will accept it. If an incorrect middle initial, spelling variant or different middle name is on the AKTR, or if the AKTR has a first name variation of any kind, the evaluator must attach an explanation and a scan or copy of the applicant's photo identification and attach it to the IACRA or paper application. If the last name on the AKTR has a different spelling or suffix, an IACRA application is not possible. The applicant must use a paper application, and the evaluator must include an explanation and copy of the applicant's photo identification to avoid a correction notice.

Appendix 4: The Practical Test – Eligibility and Prerequisites

The prerequisite requirements and general eligibility for a practical test and the specific requirements for the original issuance of a Private Pilot Certificate in the airplane category can be found in 14 CFR part 61, sections 61.39(a) (1) through (7) and 61.103.

Appendix 5: Practical Test Roles, Responsibilities, and Outcomes

Applicant Responsibilities

The applicant is responsible for mastering the established standards for knowledge, skill, and risk management elements in all Tasks appropriate to the certificate and rating sought. The applicant should use this ACS, its references, and the Practical Test Checklist in this Appendix in preparation to take the practical test.

Instructor Responsibilities

The instructor is responsible for training the applicant to meet the established standards for knowledge, skill, and risk management elements in all Tasks appropriate to the certificate and rating sought. The instructor should use this ACS and its references as part of preparing the applicant to take the practical test and, if necessary, in retraining the applicant to proficiency in all subject(s) missed on the knowledge test.

Evaluator Responsibilities

An evaluator is:

- Aviation Safety Inspector (ASI);
- Pilot examiner (other than administrative pilot examiners);
- Training center evaluator (TCE);
- Chief instructor, assistant chief instructor or check instructor of pilot school holding examining authority; or
- Instrument Flight Instructor (CFII) conducting an instrument proficiency check (IPC).

The evaluator who conducts the practical test is responsible for determining that the applicant meets the established standards of aeronautical knowledge, skills (flight proficiency), and risk management for the Tasks in the appropriate ACS. This responsibility also includes verifying the experience requirements specified for a certificate or rating.

Prior to beginning the practical test, the evaluator must also determine that the applicant meets FAA Aviation English Language Proficiency Standard. An applicant for an FAA certificate or rating should be able to communicate in English in a discernible and understandable manner with ATC, pilots, and others involved in preparing an aircraft for flight and operating an aircraft in flight. This communication may or may not involve the use of the radio. An applicant for an FAA certificate issued in accordance with part 61, 63, 65, or 107 who cannot hear or speak due to a medical deficiency may be eligible for an FAA certificate with specific operational limitations. For additional guidance, reference AC 60-28, English Language Skill Standards required by 14 CFR parts 61, 63, 65, and 107, as amended.

The evaluator must develop a Plan of Action (POA), written in English, to conduct the practical test, and it must include all of the required Areas of Operation and Tasks. The POA must include a scenario that evaluates as many of the required Areas of Operation and Tasks as possible. As the scenario unfolds during the test, the evaluator will introduce problems and emergencies that the applicant must manage. The evaluator has the discretion to modify the POA in order to accommodate unexpected situations as they arise. For example, the evaluator may elect to suspend and later resume a scenario in order to assess certain Tasks.

In the integrated ACS framework, the Areas of Operation contain Tasks that include "knowledge" elements (such as K1), "risk management" elements (such as R1), and "skill" elements (such as S1). Knowledge and risk management elements are primarily evaluated during the knowledge testing phase of the airman certification process. The evaluator must assess the applicant on all skill elements for each Task included in each Area of Operation of the ACS, unless otherwise noted. The evaluator administering the practical test has the discretion to combine Tasks/elements as appropriate to testing scenarios.

The required minimum elements to include in the POA, unless otherwise noted, from each applicable Task are as follows:

- at least one knowledge element;
- at least one risk management element;
- all skill elements; and

- any Task elements in which the applicant was shown to be deficient on the knowledge test.

Note: *Task elements added to the POA on the basis of being listed on the AKTR may satisfy the other minimum Task element requirements. The missed items on the AKTR are not required to be added in addition to the minimum Task element requirements.*

There is no expectation for testing every knowledge and risk management element in a Task, but the evaluator has discretion to sample as needed to ensure the applicant's mastery of that Task.

Unless otherwise noted in the Task, the evaluator must test each item in the skills section by asking the applicant to perform each one. As safety of flight conditions permit, the evaluator should use questions during flight to test knowledge and risk management elements not evident in the demonstrated skills. To the greatest extent practicable, evaluators should test the applicant's ability to apply and correlate information, and use rote questions only when they are appropriate for the material being tested. If the Task includes an element with sub-elements, the evaluator may choose the primary element and select at least one sub-element to satisfy the requirement that at least one knowledge element be selected. For example, if the evaluator chooses PA.I.H.K1, he or she must select a sub-element like PA.I.H.K1e to satisfy the requirement to select one knowledge element.

Possible Outcomes of the Test

There are three possible outcomes of the practical test: (1) Temporary Airman Certificate (satisfactory), (2) Notice of Disapproval (unsatisfactory), or (3) Letter of Discontinuance.

If the evaluator determines that a Task is incomplete, or the outcome is uncertain, the evaluator must require the applicant to repeat that Task, or portions of that Task. This provision does not mean that instruction, practice, or the repetition of an unsatisfactory Task is permitted during the practical test.

If the outcome is unsatisfactory, the evaluator must issue a Notice of Disapproval.

Satisfactory Performance

In accordance with 14 CFR part 61, section 61.43, satisfactory performance requires that the applicant:

- Demonstrate the Tasks specified in the Areas of Operation for the certificate or rating sought within the established standards;
- Demonstrate mastery of the aircraft by performing each Task successfully;
- Demonstrate proficiency and competency in accordance with the approved standards;
- Demonstrate sound judgment and exercise aeronautical decision-making/risk management; and

The applicant is expected to demonstrate competence in resource management (CRM/SRM) appropriate to the aircraft and Tasks.

Satisfactory performance will result in the issuance of a temporary certificate.

Unsatisfactory Performance

Typical areas of unsatisfactory performance and grounds for disqualification include:

- Any action or lack of action by the applicant that requires corrective intervention by the evaluator to maintain safe flight.
- Failure to use proper and effective visual scanning techniques to clear the area before and while performing maneuvers.
- Consistently exceeding tolerances stated in the skill elements of the Task.
- Failure to take prompt corrective action when tolerances are exceeded.
- Failure to exercise risk management.

If, in the judgment of the evaluator, the applicant does not meet the standards for any Task, the applicant fails the Task and associated Area of Operation. The test is unsatisfactory, and the evaluator issues a Notice of Disapproval. The evaluator lists the Area(s) of Operation in which the applicant did not meet the standard, any Area(s) of Operation not tested, and the number of practical test failures. The evaluator should also list the Tasks failed or Tasks not tested within any unsatisfactory or partially completed Area(s) of Operation. If the applicant's inability to meet English language requirements contributed to the failure of a Task, the evaluator must note "English Proficiency" on the Notice of Disapproval.

The evaluator or the applicant may end the test if the applicant fails a Task. The evaluator may continue the test only with the consent of the applicant. The applicant is entitled to credit only for those Areas of Operation and the associated Tasks performed satisfactorily.

Discontinuance

When it is necessary to discontinue a practical test for reasons other than unsatisfactory performance (e.g., equipment failure, weather, illness), the evaluator must return all test paperwork to the applicant. The evaluator must prepare, sign, and issue a Letter of Discontinuance that lists those Areas of Operation the applicant successfully completed and the time period remaining to complete the test. The evaluator should advise the applicant to present the Letter of Discontinuance to the evaluator when the practical test resumes in order to receive credit for the items successfully completed. The Letter of Discontinuance becomes part of the applicant's certification file.

Testing after Discontinuance or Unsatisfactory Performance

In accordance with 14 CFR part 61, section 61.39(f), a discontinued or unsatisfactory practical test cycle completes within two calendar months after the month the applicant begins the test. In addition and in accordance with section 61.43(f), an applicant may receive credit for items passed, but only within a 60-day period after the date of a first failure or Letter of Discontinuance. When an applicant is entitled to credit for Areas of Operation previously passed as indicated on a Notice of Disapproval or Letter of Discontinuance, evaluators should continue using the PTS/ACS effective on the start date of the test cycle. The evaluator has discretion to reevaluate any Task(s) successfully completed within a failed or partially tested Area of Operation.

Practical Test Checklist (Applicant)
Appointment with Evaluator

Evaluator's Name: _____

Location: _____

Date/Time: _____

Acceptable Aircraft

- ☐ Aircraft Documents:
    - ☐ Airworthiness Certificate
    - ☐ Registration Certificate
    - ☐ Operating Limitations
- ☐ Aircraft Maintenance Records:
    - ☐ Logbook Record of Airworthiness Inspections and AD Compliance
- ☐ Pilot's Operating Handbook, FAA-Approved Aircraft Flight Manual

Personal Equipment

- ☐ View-Limiting Device
- ☐ Current Aeronautical Charts (printed or electronic)
- ☐ Computer and Plotter
- ☐ Flight Plan Form and Flight Logs (printed or electronic)
- ☐ Chart Supplements, Airport Diagrams, and appropriate publications
- ☐ Current AIM

Personal Records

- ☐ Identification—Photo/Signature ID
- ☐ Pilot Certificate
- ☐ Current Medical Certificate or BasicMed qualification (when applicable)
- ☐ Completed FAA Form 8710-1, Airman Certificate and/or Rating Application with Instructor's Signature or completed IACRA form
- ☐ Original Airman Knowledge Test Report
- ☐ Pilot Logbook with appropriate Instructor Endorsements
- ☐ FAA Form 8060-5, Notice of Disapproval (if applicable)
- ☐ Letter of Discontinuance (if applicable)
- ☐ Approved School Graduation Certificate (if applicable)
- ☐ Evaluator's Fee (if applicable)

Additional Rating Task Table

For an applicant who holds at least a Private Pilot Certificate and seeks an additional airplane category and/or class rating at the private pilot level, the evaluator must evaluate that applicant in the Areas of Operation and Tasks listed in the Additional Rating Task Table. Please note, however, that the evaluator has the discretion to evaluate the applicant's competence in the remaining Areas of Operation and Tasks.

If the applicant holds two or more category or class ratings at least at the private level, and the ratings table indicates differing required Tasks, the "least restrictive" entry applies. For example, if "All" and "None" are indicated for one Area of Operation, the "None" entry applies. If "B" and "B, C" are indicated, the "B" entry applies.

Addition of an Airplane Single-Engine Land Rating to an existing Private Pilot Certificate

Required Tasks are indicated by either the Task letter(s) that apply(s) or an indication that all or none of the Tasks must be tested based on the notes in each Area of Operation.

Private Pilot Rating(s) Held

Areas of Operation	ASES	AMEL	AMES	RH	RG	Glider	Balloon	Airship
I	F,G	F,G	F,G	F,G	F,G	F,G	F,G	F,G
II	A,B,D,F	A,B,F	A,B,D,F	A,B,C,D,F	A,B,C,D,F	A,B,C,D,F	A,B,C,D,F	A,B,C,D,F
III	B	None	B	B	B	B	B	B
IV	A,B,C,D,E,F	A,B,C,D,E,F,M	A,B,C,D,E,F,M	A,B,C,D,E,F,M,N	A,B,C,D,E,F,M,N	A,B,C,D,E,F,M,N	A,B,C,D,E,F,M,N	A,B,C,D,E,F,M,N
V	None	None	None	A,B	A	A,B	A,B	A,B
VI	None	None	None	None	None	A,B,C,D	A,B,C,D	None
VII	None	None	None	All	All	All	All	All
VIII	None	None	None	A,B,C,D,E,F	A,B,C,D,E,F	A,B,C,D,E,F	A,B,C,D,E,F	A,B,C,D,E,F
IX	A,B,C	A,B,C	A,B,C	A,B,C,D	A,B,C,D	A,B,C,D	A,B,C,D	A,B,C,D
X	None	None	None	None	None	None	None	None
XI	None	None	None	None	None	A	A	A
XII	A	None	A	A	A	A	A	A

A-12

Addition of an Airplane Single-Engine Sea Rating to an existing Private Pilot Certificate

Required Tasks are indicated by either the Task letter(s) that apply(s) or an indication that all or none of the Tasks must be tested based on the notes in each Area of Operation.

Private Pilot Rating(s) Held

Areas of Operation	ASEL	AMEL	AMES	RH	RG	Glider	Balloon	Airship
I	F,G,I	F,G,I	F,G	F,G,I	F,G,I	D,F,G,I	D,F,G,I	D,F,G,I
II	A,B,E,F	A,B,E,F	A,B,,F	A,B,C,E,F	A,B,C,E,F	A,B,C,E,F	A,B,C,E,F	A,B,C,E,F
III	B	B	None	B	B	B	B	B
IV	A,B,G,H,I, J,K,L	A,B,G,H I,J,K,L,M	A,B,M	A,B,G,H,I, J,K,L,M,N	A,B,G,H,I, J,K,L,M,N	A,B,G,H,I, J,K,L,M,N	A,B,G,H,I, J,K,L,M,N	A,B,G,H,I, J,K,L,M,N
V	None	None	None	All	A	All	All	All
VI	None	None	None	None	None	All	All	None
VII	None	None	None	All	All	All	All	All
VIII	None	None	None	All	All	All	All	All
IX	None	B,C	B,C	A,B,C	A,B,C	A,B,C	A,B,C	A,B,C
X	None	None	None	None	None	None	None	None
XI	None	None	None	None	None	All	All	All
XII	B	B	None	B	B	B	B	B

A-13

Addition of an Airplane Multiengine Land Rating to an existing Private Pilot Certificate

Required Tasks are indicated by either the Task letter(s) that apply(s) or an indication that all or none of the Tasks must be tested based on the notes in each Area of Operation.

Private Pilot Rating(s) Held

Areas of Operation	ASEL	ASES	AMES	RH	RG	Glider	Balloon	Airship
I	F,G	F,G	F,G	F,G	F,G	D,F,G	D,F,G	F,G
II	A,B,C, D,F	A,B,C, D,F	A,D	A,B,C, D,F	A,B,C, D,F	A,B,C, D,F	A,B,C, D,F	A,B,C, D,F
III	None	B	B	B	B	B	B	B
IV	A,B,E,F	A,B,E,F	A,B,E,F	A,B,E, F,N	A,B,E, F,N	A,B,E, F,N	A,B,E, F,N	A,B,E, F,N
V	A	A	None	All	A	All	All	All
VI	None	None	None	None	None	All	All	None
VII	All	All	None	All	All	All	All	All
VIII	None	None	None	All	All	All	All	All
IX	E,F,G	E,F,G	None	A,C, E,F,G	A,C, E,F,G	A,C, E,F,G	A,C, E,F,G	A,C, E,F,G
X*	All	All	None	All	All	All	All	All
XI	None	None	None	None	None	A	A	A
XII	None	A	A	A	A	A	A	A

---

* Tasks C and D are not required for applicants who are instrument-rated and who have previously demonstrated instrument proficiency in a multiengine airplane or for applicants who do not hold an instrument rating.

Addition of an Airplane Multiengine Sea Rating to an existing Private Pilot Certificate

Required Tasks are indicated by either the Task letter(s) that apply(s) or an indication that all or none of the Tasks must be tested based on the notes in each Area of Operation.

Private Pilot Rating(s) Held

Areas of Operation	ASEL	ASES	AMEL	RH	RG	Glider	Balloon	Airship
I	F,G,I	F,G	F,G,I	F,G,I	F,G,I	D,F,G,I	D,F,G,I	F,G,I
II	A,B,E,F	A,B,E,F	A,B,E,F	A,B,C,E,F	A,B,C,E,F	A,B,C,E,F	A,B,C,E,F	A,B,C,E,F
III	None	None	None	B	B	B	B	B
IV	A,B,G,H, I,J,K,L	A,B	A,B,G,H, I,J,K,L	A,B,G,H,I, J,K,L,N	A,B,G,H,I, J,K,L,N	A,B,G,H,I, J,K,L,N	A,B,G,H,I, J,K,L,N	A,B,G,H,I, J,K,L,N
V	A	A	None	All	A	All	All	All
VI	None	None	None	None	None	All	All	None
VII	All	All	None	All	All	All	All	All
VIII	None	None	None	All	All	All	All	All
IX	E,F,G	E,F,G	None	A,C,E,F,G	A,C,E,F,G	A,C,E,F,G	A,C,E,F,G	A,C,E,F,G
X*	All	All	None	All	All	All	All	All
XI	None	None	None	None	None	All	All	All
XII	B	None	B	B	B	B	B	B

Note: An applicant who holds a Private Airplane Multiengine Land Rating (AMEL) without a center thrust limitation is not required to supply a seaplane with propeller feathering capability when testing to add a Private Airplane Multiengine Sea Rating (AMES).

---

* Tasks C and D are not required for applicants who are instrument-rated and who have previously demonstrated instrument proficiency in a multiengine airplane or for applicants who do not hold an instrument rating.

Removal of the "Airplane Multiengine VFR Only" Limitation

The removal of the "Airplane Multiengine VFR Only" limitation, at the private pilot certificate level, requires an applicant to satisfactorily perform the following Area of Operation and Tasks from the Private Pilot – Airplane ACS in a multiengine airplane that has a manufacturer's published V_{MC} speed.

X.	Multiengine Operations
Task C:	Engine Failure During Flight (by Reference to Instruments) (AMEL, AMES)
Task D:	Instrument Approach and Landing with an Inoperative Engine (Simulated) (by Reference to Instruments) (AMEL, AMES)

Removal of the "Limited to Center Thrust" Limitation

The "Limited to Center Thrust" limitation for the AMEL rating is issued to applicants who complete the practical test for the AMEL rating in an aircraft that does not have a manufacturer's published V_{MC}. When conducting a practical test for the purpose of removing the "Limited to Center Thrust" limitation from the AMEL rating, the applicant must be tested on the multiengine Tasks identified in the table below in a multiengine airplane that has a manufacturer's published V_{MC} speed. This speed would be found on the type certificate data sheet (TCDS) or in the AFM. If the limitation will be removed under parts 121, 135, or 142, it must be done in accordance with an approved curriculum or training program. An applicant who holds an airplane instrument rating and has not demonstrated instrument proficiency in a multiengine airplane with a published V_{MC} shall complete the additional Tasks listed under Removal of the "Airplane Multiengine VFR Only" Limitation section.

IX.	Emergency Operations
Task E:	Engine Failure During Takeoff Before V_{MC} (Simulated) (AMEL and AMES)
Task F:	Engine Failure After Liftoff (Simulated) (AMEL, AMES)
Task G:	Approach and Landing with an Inoperative Engine (Simulated) (AMEL, AMES)
X.	**Multiengine Operations**
Task A:	Maneuvering with One Engine Inoperative (AMEL, AMES)
Task B:	V_{MC} Demonstration (AMEL and AMES)

Appendix 6: Safety of Flight

General

Safety of flight must be the prime consideration at all times. The evaluator, applicant, and crew must be constantly alert for other traffic. If performing aspects of a given maneuver, such as emergency procedures, would jeopardize safety, the evaluator will ask the applicant to simulate that portion of the maneuver. The evaluator will assess the applicant's use of visual scanning and collision avoidance procedures throughout the entire test.

Stall and Spin Awareness

During flight training and testing, the applicant and the instructor or evaluator must always recognize and avoid operations that could lead to an inadvertent stall or spin and inadvertent loss of control.

Use of Checklists

Throughout the practical test, the applicant is evaluated on the use of an appropriate checklist.

Assessing proper checklist use depends upon the specific Task. In all cases, the evaluator should determine whether the applicant appropriately divides attention and uses proper visual scanning. In some situations, reading the actual checklist may be impractical or unsafe. In such cases, the evaluator should assess the applicant's performance of published or recommended immediate action "memory" items along with his or her review of the appropriate checklist once conditions permit.

In a single-pilot airplane, the applicant should demonstrate the crew resource management (CRM) principles described as single-pilot resource management (SRM). Proper use is dependent on the specific Task being evaluated. The situation may be such that the use of the checklist while accomplishing elements of an Objective would be either unsafe or impractical in a single-pilot operation. In this case, a review of the checklist after the elements have been accomplished is appropriate.

Use of Distractions

Numerous studies indicate that many accidents have occurred when the pilot has been distracted during critical phases of flight. The evaluator should incorporate realistic distractions during the flight portion of the practical test to evaluate the pilot's situational awareness and ability to utilize proper control technique while dividing attention both inside and outside the cockpit.

Positive Exchange of Flight Controls

There must always be a clear understanding of who has control of the aircraft. Prior to flight, the pilots involved should conduct a briefing that includes reviewing the procedures for exchanging flight controls.

The FAA recommends a positive three-step process for exchanging flight controls between pilots:

- When one pilot seeks to have the other pilot take control of the aircraft, he or she will say, "You have the flight controls."
- The second pilot acknowledges immediately by saying, "I have the flight controls."
- The first pilot again says, "You have the flight controls," and visually confirms the exchange.

Pilots should follow this procedure during any exchange of flight controls, including any occurrence during the practical test. The FAA also recommends that both pilots use a visual check to verify that the exchange has occurred. There must never be any doubt as to who is flying the aircraft.

Aeronautical Decision-Making, Risk Management, Crew Resource Management and Single-Pilot Resource Management

Throughout the practical test, the evaluator must assess the applicant's ability to use sound aeronautical decision-making procedures in order to identify hazards and mitigate risk. The evaluator must accomplish this requirement by reference to the risk management elements of the given Task(s), and by developing scenarios that incorporate and combine Tasks appropriate to assessing the applicant's risk management in making safe aeronautical decisions. For example, the evaluator may develop a scenario that incorporates weather decisions and performance planning.

In assessing the applicant's performance, the evaluator should take note of the applicant's use of CRM and, if appropriate, SRM. CRM/SRM is the set of competencies that includes situational awareness, communication skills, teamwork, task allocation, and decision-making within a comprehensive framework of standard operating procedures (SOP). SRM specifically refers to the management of all resources onboard the aircraft as well as outside resources available to the single pilot.

Deficiencies in CRM/SRM almost always contribute to the unsatisfactory performance of a Task. While evaluation of CRM/SRM may appear to be somewhat subjective, the evaluator should use the risk management elements of the given Task(s) to determine whether the applicant's performance of the Task(s) demonstrates both understanding and application of the associated risk management elements.

Multiengine Considerations

On multiengine practical tests, where the failure of the most critical engine after liftoff is required, the evaluator must consider local atmospheric conditions, terrain, and type of aircraft used. The evaluator must not simulate failure of an engine until attaining at least $V_{SSE}/V_{XSE}/V_{YSE}$ and an altitude not lower than 400 feet AGL.

The applicant must supply an airplane that does not prohibit the demonstration of feathering the propeller in flight. However, an applicant holding an unrestricted AMEL rating may take a practical test for the addition of an AMES rating in an AMES without propeller feathering capability. Practical tests conducted in a flight simulation training device (FSTD) can only be accomplished as part of an approved curriculum or training program. Any limitations or powerplant failure will be noted in that program.

For safety reasons, when the practical test is conducted in an airplane, the applicant must perform Tasks that require feathering or shutdown only under conditions and at a position and altitude where it is possible to make a safe landing on an established airport if there is difficulty in unfeathering the propeller or restarting the engine. The evaluator must select an entry altitude that will allow the single-engine demonstration Tasks to be completed no lower than 3,000 feet AGL or the manufacturer's recommended altitude (whichever is higher). If it is not possible to unfeather the propeller or restart the engine while airborne, the applicant and the evaluator should treat the situation as an emergency. At altitudes lower than 3,000 feet AGL, engine failure should be simulated by reducing throttle to idle and then establishing zero thrust.

Engine failure (simulated) during takeoff should be accomplished prior to reaching 50 percent of the calculated V_{MC}.

Single-Engine Considerations

For safety reasons, the evaluator will not request a simulated powerplant failure in a single-engine airplane unless it is possible to safely complete a landing.

High-Performance Airplane Considerations

In some high-performance airplanes, the power setting may have to be reduced below the ACS guidelines power setting to prevent excessively high pitch attitudes greater than 30° nose up.

Appendix 7: Aircraft, Equipment, and Operational Requirements & Limitations

Aircraft Requirements & Limitations

14 CFR part 61, section 61.45 prescribes the required aircraft and equipment for a practical test. The regulation states the minimum aircraft registration and airworthiness requirements as well as the minimum equipment requirements, to include the minimum required controls.

Multiengine practical tests require normal engine shutdowns and restarts in the air, to include propeller feathering and unfeathering. The Airplane Flight Manual (AFM) must not prohibit these procedures, but low power settings for cooling periods prior to the actual shutdown in accordance with the AFM are acceptable and encouraged. For a type rating in an airplane not certificated with inflight unfeathering capability, a simulated powerplant failure is acceptable.

If the multiengine airplane used for the practical test does not publish a V_{MC}, then the "Limited to Centerline Thrust" limitation will be added to the certificate issued from this check, unless the applicant has previously demonstrated competence in a multiengine airplane with a published V_{MC}.

If the aircraft presented for the practical test has inoperative instruments or equipment, it must be addressed in accordance with 14 CFR part 91, section 91.213. If the aircraft can be operated in accordance with 14 CFR part 91, section 91.213, then it must be determined if the inoperative instruments or equipment are required to complete the practical test.

Equipment Requirements & Limitations

The equipment examination should be administered before the flight portion of the practical test, but it must be closely coordinated and related to the flight portion.

The aircraft must meet the requirements as outlined in 14 CFR part 61, section 61.45.

To assist in management of the aircraft during the practical test, the applicant is expected to demonstrate automation management skills by utilizing installed, available, or airborne equipment such as autopilot, avionics and systems displays, and/or a flight management system (FMS). The evaluator is expected to test the applicant's knowledge of the systems that are available or installed and operative during both the ground and flight portions of the practical test. If the applicant has trained using a portable EFB to display charts and data, and wishes to use the EFB during the practical test, the applicant is expected to demonstrate appropriate knowledge, risk management, and skill.

If the practical test is conducted in an aircraft, the applicant is required by 14 CFR part 61, section 61.45(d)(2) to provide an appropriate view limiting device acceptable to the evaluator. The applicant and the evaluator should establish a procedure as to when and how this device should be donned and removed, and brief this procedure before the flight. The device must be used during all testing that requires flight "solely by reference to instruments" included as part of the Task objective. This device must prevent the applicant from having visual reference outside the aircraft, but it must not restrict the evaluator's ability to see and avoid other traffic. The use of the device does not apply to specific elements within a Task when there is a requirement for visual references.

Operational Requirements, Limitations, & Task Information

V. Performance and Ground Reference Maneuvers

Task B. Ground Reference Maneuvers

As noted in the skill elements, the evaluator must choose at least one maneuver for the applicant to demonstrate:

- Rectangular course
- S-Turns
- Turns around a point

VII. Slow Flight and Stalls

Task A. Maneuvering During Slow Flight

A-19

Evaluation criteria for this Task should recognize that environmental factors (e.g., turbulence) may result in a momentary activation of stall warning indicators such as the stall horn. If the applicant recognizes the stall warning indication and promptly makes an appropriate correction, a momentary activation does not constitute unsatisfactory performance on this Task. As with other Tasks, unsatisfactory performance would arise from an applicant's continual deviation from the standard, lack of correction, and/or lack of recognition.

Task B. Power-Off Stalls

Evaluation criteria for a recovery from an approach to stall should not mandate a predetermined value for altitude loss and should not mandate maintaining altitude during recovery. Proper evaluation criteria should consider the multitude of external and internal variables that affect the recovery altitude.

Task C. Power-On Stalls

In some high-performance airplanes, the power setting may have to be reduced below the ACS guidelines power setting to prevent excessively high pitch attitudes greater than 30° nose up. Evaluation criteria for a recovery from an approach to stall should not mandate a predetermined value for altitude loss and should not mandate maintaining altitude during recovery. Proper evaluation criteria should consider the multitude of external and internal variables that affect the recovery altitude.

IX. Emergency Operations

Task E. Engine Failure During Takeoff Before V_{MC} (Simulated) (AMEL, AMES)

Engine failure (simulated) during takeoff should be accomplished prior to reaching 50 percent of the calculated V_{MC}.

X. Multiengine Operations

Task B. V_{MC} Demonstration (AMEL, AMES)

Airplanes with normally aspirated engines will lose power as altitude increases because of the reduced density of the air entering the induction system of the engine. This loss of power will result in a V_{MC} lower than the stall speed at higher altitudes. Therefore, recovery should be made at the first indication of loss of directional control, stall warning, or buffet. Do not perform this maneuver by increasing the pitch attitude to a high angle with both engines operating and then reducing power on the critical engine. This technique is hazardous and may result in loss of airplane control.

Task C. Engine Failure During Flight (by Reference to Instruments) (AMEL, AMES)

This Task is not required if an instrument-rated applicant has previously demonstrated instrument proficiency in a multiengine airplane, or if the applicant does not hold an Instrument Airplane Rating. If an applicant holds both a single- and multiengine rating on a pilot certificate, but has not demonstrated instrument proficiency in a multiengine aircraft, that airman's certificate must bear a limitation indicating that multiengine flight is permitted in visual flight rules (VFR) conditions only.

Task D. Instrument Approach and Landing with an Inoperative Engine (Simulated) (by Reference to Instruments) (AMEL, AMES)

This Task is not required if an instrument-rated applicant has previously demonstrated instrument proficiency in a multiengine airplane, or if the applicant does not hold an Instrument Airplane Rating. If an applicant holds both a single- and multiengine rating on a pilot certificate, but has not demonstrated instrument proficiency in a multiengine aircraft, that airman's certificate must bear a limitation indicating that multiengine flight is permitted in visual flight rules (VFR) conditions only.

Appendix 8: Use of Flight Simulation Training Devices (FSTD) and Aviation Training Devices (ATD): Airplane Single-Engine, Multiengine Land and Sea

Use of Flight Simulator Training Devices

14 CFR part 61, section 61.4, *Qualification and approval of flight simulators and flight training devices*, states in paragraph (a) that each full flight simulator (FFS) and flight training device (FTD) used for training, and for which an airman is to receive credit to satisfy any training, testing, or checking requirement under this chapter, must be qualified and approved by the Administrator for—

> *(1) the training, testing, and checking for which it is used;*

> *(2) each particular maneuver, procedure, or crewmember function performed; and*

> *(3) the representation of the specific category and class of aircraft, type of aircraft, particular variation within the type of aircraft, or set of aircraft for certain flight training devices.*

14 CFR part 60 prescribes the rules governing the initial and continuing qualification and use of all Flight Simulator Training Devices (FSTD) used for meeting training, evaluation, or flight experience requirements for flight crewmember certification or qualification.

An FSTD is defined in 14 CFR part 60 as an FFS or FTD:

> **Full Flight Simulator (FFS)**—*a replica of a specific type, make, model, or series aircraft. It includes the equipment and computer programs necessary to represent aircraft operations in ground and flight conditions, a visual system providing an out-of-the-flight deck view, a system that provides cues at least equivalent to those of a three-degree-of-freedom motion system, and has the full range of capabilities of the systems installed in the device as described in part 60 of this chapter and the qualification performance standard (QPS) for a specific FFS qualification level. (part 1)*

> **Flight Training Device (FTD)**—*a replica of aircraft instruments, equipment, panels, and controls in an open flight deck area or an enclosed aircraft flight deck replica. It includes the equipment and computer programs necessary to represent aircraft (or set of aircraft) operations in ground and flight conditions having the full range of capabilities of the systems installed in the device as described in part 60 of this chapter and the QPS for a specific FTD qualification level (part 1).*

The FAA National Simulator Program (NSP) qualifies Level A-D FFSs and Level 4 – 7[1] FTDs. In addition, each operational rule part identifies additional requirements for the approval and use of FSTDs in a training program[2]. Use of an FSTD for the completion of the private pilot airplane practical test is permitted only when accomplished in accordance with an FAA approved curriculum or training program.

Use of Aviation Training Devices

14 CFR part 61, section 61.4(c) states the Administrator may approve a device other than an FFS or FTD for specific purposes. Under this authority, the FAA's General Aviation and Commercial Division provides approvals for aviation training devices (ATD).

---

[1]The FSTD qualification standards in effect prior to part 60 defined a Level 7 FTD for airplanes (see Advisory Circular 120-45A, Airplane Flight Training Device Qualification, 1992). This device required high fidelity, airplane specific aerodynamic and flight control models similar to a Level D FFS, but did not require a motion cueing system or visual display system. In accordance with the "grandfather rights" of 14 CFR part 60, section 60.17, these previously qualified devices will retain their qualification basis as long as they continue to meet the standards under which they were originally qualified. There is only one airplane Level 7 FTD with grandfather rights that remains in the U.S. As a result of changes to part 60 that were published in the Federal Register in March 2016, the airplane Level 7 FTD was reinstated with updated evaluation standards. The new Level 7 FTD will require a visual display system for qualification. The minimum qualified Tasks for the Level 7 FTD are described in Table B1B of Appendix B of part 60.

[2] 14 CFR part 121, section 121.407; part 135, section 135.335; part 141, section 141.41; and part 142, section 142.59.

Advisory Circular (AC) 61-136A, *FAA Approval of Aviation Training Devices and Their Use for Training and Experience,* provides information and guidance for the required function, performance, and effective use of ATDs for pilot training and aeronautical experience (including instrument currency). FAA issues a letter of authorization (LOA) to an ATD manufacturer approving an ATD as a basic aviation training device (BATD) or an advanced aviation training device (AATD). LOAs are valid for a five-year period with a specific expiration date and include the amount of credit a pilot may take for training and experience requirements.

> *Aviation Training Device (ATD)—a training device, other than an FFS or FTD, that has been evaluated, qualified, and approved by the Administrator. In general, this includes a replica of aircraft instruments, equipment, panels, and controls in an open flight deck area or an enclosed aircraft cockpit. It includes the hardware and software necessary to represent a category and class of aircraft (or set of aircraft) operations in ground and flight conditions having the appropriate range of capabilities and systems installed in the device as described within AC 61-136 for the specific basic or advanced qualification level.*

> *Basic Aviation Training Device (BATD)—provides an adequate training platform for both procedural and operational performance Tasks specific to instrument experience and the ground and flight training requirements for the Private Pilot Certificate and Instrument Rating per 14 CFR parts 61 and 141.*

> *Advanced Aviation Training Device (AATD)—provides an adequate training platform for both procedural and operational performance Tasks specific to the ground and flight training requirements for the Private Pilot Certificate, Instrument Rating Certificate, Commercial Pilot Certificate, Airline Transport Pilot Certificate, and Flight Instructor Certificate per 14 CFR parts 61 and 141. It also provides an adequate platform for Tasks required for instrument experience and the instrument proficiency check.*

Note: *ATDs cannot be used for practical tests, aircraft type specific training, or for an aircraft type rating; therefore use of an ATD for the private pilot airplane practical test is not permitted.*

Credit for Time in an FSTD

14 CFR part 61, section 61.109 specifies the minimum aeronautical experience requirements for a person applying for a Private Pilot Certificate. Paragraphs (a) and (b) specify the time requirements for a Private Pilot Certificate in a single-engine airplane and a multiengine airplane, respectively[3]. These paragraphs include specific experience requirements that must be completed in an airplane. Paragraph (k) of this section specifies the amount of credit a pilot can take for time in an FFS or FTD. For those that received training in programs outside of 14 CFR part 142, section 61.109(k)(1)[4] applies. For those pilots that received training through a 14 CFR part 142 program, section 61.109(k)(2) applies.

Credit for Time in an ATD

14 CFR part 61, section 61.109 specifies the minimum aeronautical experience requirements for a person applying for a private pilot certificate Paragraphs (a) and (b) specify the time requirements for a private pilot certificate in a single-engine airplane and a multiengine airplane, respectively[5]. These paragraphs include specific experience requirements that must be completed in an airplane. Paragraph (k) of this section specifies the amount of credit a pilot can take towards the private pilot certificate aeronautical experience requirements.

In order to credit pilot time, an ATD must be FAA-approved and the time must be provided by an authorized instructor. AC 61-136A, states the LOA for each approved ATD will indicate the credit allowances for pilot training and experience, as provided under 14 CFR parts 61 and 141. Time with an instructor in a BATD and an AATD may be credited towards the aeronautical experience requirements for the private pilot certificate as specified in the LOA for the device used. It is recommended that applicants who intend to take credit for time in a BATD or an AATD towards the aeronautical experience requirements for the private pilot certificate obtain a copy of the LOA for each device used so they have a record for how much credit may be taken. For additional information on the logging of ATD time, reference AC 61-136A.

---

[3] The minimum aeronautical experience requirements may be further reduced as permitted in 14 CFR part 61, section 61.109(k)(3).

[4] As part of program approval, 14 CFR part 141 training providers must also adhere to the requirements for permitted time in an FFS or FTD per Appendix B to 14 CFR part 141.

[5] The minimum aeronautical experience requirements may be further reduced as permitted in 14 CFR part 61, section 61.109(k)(3).

Use of an FSTD on a Practical Test

14 CFR part 61, section 61.45 specifies the required aircraft and equipment that must be provided for a practical test unless permitted to use an FFS or FTD for the flight portion. 14 CFR part, section 61.64 provides the criteria for using an FSTD for a practical test. Specifically, paragraph (a) states –

> *If an applicant for a certificate or rating uses a flight simulator or flight training device for training or any portion of the practical test, the flight simulator and flight training device—*
>
> *(1) Must represent the category, class, and type (if a type rating is applicable) for the rating sought; and*
>
> *(2) Must be qualified and approved by the Administrator and used in accordance with an approved course of training under 14 CFR part 141 or part 142 of this chapter; or under 14 CFR part 121 or part 135 of this chapter, provided the applicant is a pilot employee of that air carrier operator.*

Therefore, practical tests or portions thereof, when accomplished in an FSTD, may only be conducted by FAA aviation safety inspectors (ASI), aircrew program designees (APD) authorized to conduct such tests in FSTDs in 14 CFR parts 121 or 135, qualified personnel and designees authorized to conduct such tests in FSTDs for 14 CFR part 141 pilot school graduates, or appropriately authorized 14 CFR part 142 Training Center Evaluators (TCE).

In addition, 14 CFR part, 61 section 61.64(b) states if an airplane is not used during the practical test for a type rating for a turbojet airplane (except for preflight inspection), an applicant must accomplish the entire practical test in a Level C or higher FFS and the applicant must meet the specific experience criteria listed. If the experience criteria cannot be met, the applicant can either—

> *(f)(1) [...] complete the following Tasks on the practical test in an aircraft appropriate to category, class, and type for the rating sought: Preflight inspection, normal takeoff, normal instrument landing system approach, missed approach, and normal landing; or*
>
> *(f)(2) The applicant's pilot certificate will be issued with a limitation that states: "The [name of the additional type rating] is subject to pilot-in-command limitations," and the applicant is restricted from serving as pilot-in-command in an aircraft of that type.*

When flight Tasks are accomplished in an airplane, certain Task elements may be accomplished through "simulated" actions in the interest of safety and practicality. However, when accomplished in an FFS or FTD, these same actions would not be "simulated." For example, when in an airplane, a simulated engine fire may be addressed by retarding the throttle to idle, simulating the shutdown of the engine, simulating the discharge of the fire suppression agent, if applicable, and simulating the disconnection of associated electrical, hydraulic, and pneumatics systems. However, when the same emergency condition is addressed in an FSTD, all Task elements must be accomplished as would be expected under actual circumstances.

Similarly, safety of flight precautions taken in the airplane for the accomplishment of a specific maneuver or procedure (such as limiting altitude in an approach to stall or setting maximum airspeed for an engine failure expected to result in a rejected takeoff) need not be taken when an FSTD is used. It is important to understand that, whether accomplished in an airplane or FSTD, all Tasks and elements for each maneuver or procedure must have the same performance standards applied equally for determination of overall satisfactory performance.

Appendix 9: References

This ACS is based on the following 14 CFR parts, FAA guidance documents, manufacturer's publications, and other documents.

Reference	Title
14 CFR part 39	Airworthiness Directives
14 CFR part 43	Maintenance, Preventive Maintenance, Rebuilding and Alteration
14 CFR part 61	Certification: Pilots, Flight Instructors, and Ground Instructors
14 CFR part 68	Requirements for Operating Certain Small Aircraft Without a Medical Certificate
14 CFR part 71	Designation of Class A, B, C, D and E Airspace Areas; Air Traffic Service Routes; and Reporting Points
14 CFR part 91	General Operating and Flight Rules
14 CFR part 93	Special Air Traffic Rules
AC 00-6	Aviation Weather
AC 00-45	Aviation Weather Services
AC 60-28	English Language Skill Standards Required by 14 CFR parts 61, 63, 65, and 107
AC 61-67	Stall and Spin Awareness Training
AC 91-73	Parts 91 and 135 Single Pilot, Flight School Procedures During Taxi Operations
AC 68-1	Alternative Pilot Physical Examination and Education Requirements
AC 91.21-1	Use of Portable Electronic Devices Aboard Aircraft
AIM	Aeronautical Information Manual
FAA-H-8083-1	Aircraft Weight and Balance Handbook
FAA-H-8083-2	Risk Management Handbook
FAA-H-8083-3	Airplane Flying Handbook
FAA-H-8083-6	Advanced Avionics Handbook
FAA-H-8083-15	Instrument Flying Handbook
FAA-H-8083-23	Seaplane, Skiplane, and Float/Ski Equipped Helicopter Operations Handbook
FAA-H-8083-25	Pilot's Handbook of Aeronautical Knowledge
FAA-P-8740-66	Flying Light Twins Safely Pamphlet
POH/AFM	Pilot's Operating Handbook/FAA-Approved Airplane Flight Manual
Other	Chart Supplements
	Navigation Charts
	Navigation Equipment Manual
	USCG Navigation Rules, International-Inland
	NOTAMs

Note: Users should reference the current edition of the reference documents listed above. The current edition of all FAA publications can be found at www.faa.gov.

Appendix 10: Abbreviations and Acronyms

The following abbreviations and acronyms are used in the ACS.

Abb./Acronym	Definition
14 CFR	Title 14 of the Code of Federal Regulations
AATD	Advanced Aviation Training Device
AC	Advisory Circular
ACS	Airman Certification Standards
AD	Airworthiness Directive
ADM	Aeronautical Decision-Making
AELS	Aviation English Language Standard
AFM	Airplane Flight Manual
AFS	Flight Standards Service
AGL	Above Ground Level
AIM	Aeronautical Information Manual
AKTR	Airman Knowledge Test Report
AMEL	Airplane Multiengine Land
AMES	Airplane Multiengine Sea
APD	Aircrew Program Designee
ASEL	Airplane Single-Engine Land
ASES	Airplane Single-Engine Sea
ASI	Aviation Safety Inspector
ATC	Air Traffic Control
ATD	Aviation Training Device
BATD	Basic Aviation Training Device
CFIT	Controlled Flight Into Terrain
CFR	Code of Federal Regulations
CG	Center of Gravity
CRM	Crew Resource Management
DA	Decision Altitude
DH	Decision Height
DPE	Designated Pilot Examiner
ELT	Emergency Locator Transmitter
ETA	Estimated Time of Arrival
FAA	Federal Aviation Administration
FFS	Full Flight Simulator
FMS	Flight Management System
FSDO	Flight Standards District Office
FSTD	Flight Simulation Training Device
FTD	Flight Training Device
ICAO	International Civil Aviation Organization
IFO	International Field Office
IFU	International Field Unit
IPC	Instrument Proficiency Check

A-25